AN INTRODUCTION TO
TEILHARD DE CHARDIN

N. M. WILDIERS

AN INTRODUCTION TO
TEILHARD DE CHARDIN

TRANSLATED BY HUBERT HOSKINS

Preface by
Christopher F. Mooney, s.j.

HARPER & ROW, PUBLISHERS

NEW YORK AND EVANSTON

This translation is made from *Teilhard de Chardin: Een inleiding in zijn denken* published in 1963 by N. V. Standaard-Boek-handel Uitgeversmaatschappij, Antwerp-Amsterdam, and subsequently revised for the English edition by the author.

English-language version first published by Fontana Books, London, and Harper & Row, New York, 1968.

Nihil Obstat John M. T. Barton STD, LSS Censor
Imprimatur ✠ Patrick Casey Vic. Gen.
Westminster, 15 September 1967

The *Nihil Obstat* and *Imprimatur* are a declaration that a book or pamphlet is considered to be free from doctrinal or moral error. It is not implied that those who have granted the *Nihil Obstat* and *Imprimatur* agree with the contents, opinions or statements expressed.

LIBRARY OF CONGRESS CATALOG CARD NUMBER: 68-17593

D-U

FOREWORD

This book represents an attempt to formulate a modest synthesis of what might be called the world of ideas created by Teilhard de Chardin. In writing it I have tried to make luminously clear the great degree of unity which marks his thinking—a unity that readily becomes apparent as soon as one realises what the central problem was which dominated his whole life and work.

Teilhard de Chardin's thought bears upon many problems in the natural sciences, philosophy and theology, and even upon some of a purely methodological character. I have not set out to state all these issues in so many words, nor yet to enter into critical discussion of the solutions which Teilhard proposed regarding them. The present work is not addressed to professional scholars or scientists but to the non-specialist reader who wishes to know something of the opinions and insights of one of the most remarkable scientists and thinkers of our century.

CONTENTS

AN INTRODUCTION TO
TEILHARD DE CHARDIN

PREFACE

by CHRISTOPHER F. MOONEY, S.J.

For about eight years the present volume has been providing readers of many European countries with what is perhaps the best short introduction to the thought of Pierre Teilhard de Chardin. Its translation into English is thus a welcome event. To begin Teilhard without a guide of some sort can be both confusing and discouraging. Yet the average person, curious about Teilhard's impact on the modern world, usually has neither time nor patience to grapple with the complexities of those full-length studies which have recently appeared in English. N. M. Wildiers has managed to avoid much of this complexity, without at the same time falling into that superficiality which characterizes most other brief treatments. He was in a good position to do this. Thoroughly familiar with all of Teilhard's writings for many years, Wildiers has since 1955 introduced each new volume of the complete works as it makes its appearance in the definitive French edition. He is moreover a theologian by profession, and this has enabled him more easily to give proper weight to the religious dimension of Teilhard's thought, a dimension most clearly discernible in essays which will not be available in English for some years.

My own remarks here are intended merely as an orientation for the uninitiated English reader. I might point out at the start that "Teilhard" (pronounced tay*ahr*) is the original family name, "de Chardin" having been added by Pierre's paternal grandfather when he married into the de Chardin family and hence into nobility. He is therefore correctly referred to either as Teilhard or Teilhard de Chardin, but not as de Chardin. Aside from formal occasions his own signature was usually Pierre Teilhard. This said, and with one's interest whetted by an introduction such as the present one, what is one to do next? How is one to pursue Teilhard further? Perhaps what is most essential is to be aware of Teilhard's perspective and general purpose in any given piece of writing. These in fact vary considerably, and ignorance of what to look for in what one reads is perhaps the greatest single source of misunderstanding for the neophyte. What follow, then, are some suggestions on how to go about reading what has appeared in English so far, as well as what to look for as one reads.

The best way to begin is naturally with the man himself, his deepest feelings, hopes and ambitions. These are vividly presented in *The Making of a Mind* (London and New York, Collins and Harper and Row, 1965), a collection of letters written to his cousin in Paris from the trenches of the first world war. Here one finds all the problems Teilhard will struggle with for the rest of his life, his need of an absolute, his love of the world and his devotion to Christ, his extreme sensitivity to the rupture between science and religion, above all his sense of mission. For what he dedicated himself to during these war years was to reconcile modern man with God by showing him that God alone gives ultimate meaning to his unquenchable desire to build the earth, and that Christianity, far from opposing this earthly ideal, gives to it greater substance and strength. " I am more keenly aware that for the rest of my life my task is to develop in myself, humbly, faithfully, doggedly—and at the same time to impart it as much as possible to others—that form of spirituality which makes one seek passionately for God in every single thing and in all one's activity."

These early letters make it clear how essential was the place of Christianity in the evolutionary system which was to develop in the years ahead. Teilhard's eventual synthesis of science and religion could never have taken place had not his thinking been polarized from the very start by the two apparently opposed concepts of God and the world. This became quite evident during the years between 1920 and his death in 1955; and at this point the reader might like to dip into the short biography by Robert Speaight, *Teilhard de Chardin,*

(London and New York, Collins and Harper and Row, 1967) or the much longer life by Claude Cuénot, *Teilhard de Chardin,* (London and Baltimore, Burns Oates and Helicon, 1965). During these years his writings were directed to the two very different groups represented by his two polar ideas, God and the world. He wanted to reach both those who believed only in heaven and those who believed only in the earth, and he felt that he was in a unique position to do so. Here is what he wrote in a 1934 essay:

> The originality of my belief is to be found in the fact that it is rooted in two domains of life usually considered antagonistic. Through my education and intellectual formation, I belong to the " children of heaven," while by temperament and owing to my professional studies I am " a child of earth." Situated by circumstances at the heart of two worlds with whose theoretical positions, language, and sentiments I am well acquainted through long experience, I have thus not tried to erect any walls between these two areas in my interior life . . . I have found that far from destroying each other, each has served to reinforce the other. To-day I probably believe more in God than ever,—and I certainly believe more than ever in the world. Do we not perhaps find here, in terms of the life of a single individual, the outline of a solution to the spiritual problem which at present most disturbs the vanguard of a humanity?

I would strongly recommend that the reader approaching the body of Teilhard's writing for the first time begin with *The Divine Milieu** (London and New York, Collins and Harper and Row, 1960). This is the chief work written for the second of the two audiences mentioned above, that of Christian believers. Unless one has read this first, it is impossible to understand the full intent of *The Phenomenon of*

---

* The English edition (Collins) is entitled *Le Milieu Divin.*

Man or the spirit with which Teilhard undertook all his scientific inquiry. For him the key to evolution was the presence and action of God in the world and more particularly the presence and action of Christ. " For a long time now," he wrote to a friend in 1936, " my chief interest in life has been to bring about in some way a plainer disclosing of God in the world." The title, divine Milieu, is in fact a Teilhardian name for Christ, since the French word *milieu*, unlike its customary English usage, denotes not simply an environment or set of influences, but their centre and source as well. And the key to his evolutionary system is the postulate of a centre of convergence for the cosmic process, a centre which must indeed be divine and transcendent if the process itself is not eventually to end in total death and therefore in absurdity. Hence the importance for believer and non-believer alike to recognize that Christianity is in no sense unconcerned with human progress, but on the contrary obliges the Christian to collaborate in furthering this progress of man by the faithful performance of all the duties of his state in life. " The great danger people see in Christianity, the great suspicion it raises in their minds, is that it tends to extinguish in its followers enthusiasm for developing the world." Teilhard wanted to dispel this impression once and for all and this he does in the first part of *The Divine Milieu*.

But there was likewise a deep need in Teilhard's life to give himself completely to God, to possess Him and be possessed by Him in the full tradition of both eastern and western mysticism. This means first of all abandoning oneself to the mystery of God's presence in that suffering and death which sooner or later must touch every human life. Such a " divinization of our passivities," as Teilhard calls it, forms the second part of *The Divine Milieu*, and seeks to orient the Christian toward the inevitability of physical evil in evolution by pointing once more to this hidden action of God at the centre of human life. This mystical orientation of Teilhard's thought is seen in an even more striking way in the last part of *The Divine Milieu*, where he eloquently explains how he understands the omnipresence of Christ in the world. A similar concern for this divine presence is the major theme of three brief essays collected together under the title *Hymn of the Universe* (London and New York, Collins and Harper and Row, 1965). The reader will find here perhaps the best example of Teilhard's spiritual writing, especially the beautiful "Mass on the World". He will likewise become aware of how important the Eucharist is for Teilhard, not only as the centre of his own spiritual life as a priest, but also as the focus of that unity between God and the material world which points to that ultimate transformation of matter seen by Teilhard as the goal of evolution.

The three books mentioned thus far will give the reader an excellent framework within which to situate Teilhard's evolutionary system. The slim volume entitled *Man's Place in Nature* (London and New York, Collins and Harper and Row, 1966) might serve as the best beginning. Planned in 1949 as a series of five lectures to summarize the main argument of the first three books of *The Phenomenon of Man*, this much shorter work provides perhaps the clearest statement of Teilhard's understanding of the evolutionary process, the skeletal outline as it were of how modern man should look upon life. He must recognize "that life is not a peculiar anomaly, sporadically flowering on matter, but a privileged amplification of a universal cosmic property, not an epiphenomenon, but the very essence of the phenomenon." Life in fact presents itself as an interiorizing, centring movement of greater and greater complexity, developing from the unarranged to the arranged, the drive being externally toward greater complexity and internally toward higher consciousness. Complexity and consciousness thus become the measure of the degree of vitalization. Only in man, however, does "consciousness", a word which Teilhard applies even to the most rudimentary form of interior perception, cross the threshold into reflection, and this is accompanied by the most complex of all known organisms, the human brain. Only in man, then, does the phenomenon of life find its fullest expression, the nucleus of the interiorizing movement of cosmic evolution.

After finishing *Man's Place in Nature*, the reader will find that he has been rather painlessly accustomed to much of Teilhard's vocabulary. He will see too that many of the unusual words, such as " cosmogenesis " and " noosphere ", introduce ideas which are quite new, while others, like " hominization " and " Omega Point ", are simply more congenial to Teilhard, allowing him to speak of his own view of the world with greater facility. Most important of all the reader will be able to handle intelligently the richly detailed development of the same material in *The Phenomenon of Man*. This is, of course, Teilhard's masterpiece, the manuscript he laboured over and revised and discussed for over ten years, only to realize finally that it would never be published in his lifetime. What he aimed at was a synthetic view of man which would enable him to grasp in a single movement the data of science and the data of Christian revelation. This meant beginning with a phenomenological analysis of the universe which, through Christian faith, he knew was oriented toward God. The natural history of the world sketched at the start thus moves into a philosophy of nature and eventually into a consideration of the problem of God. To understand Teilhard's motivation here it would be well at this point briefly to consider the problem which preoccupied him while writing *The Phenomenon of Man* and for many years afterward.

Why, he asked himself, is there to be found in our own time a hitherto unknown amalgam of anxieties and hopes bringing such restless uneasiness to both individuals and nations? The answer he felt was to be found in the gradual increase over the centuries of interiority and human freedom, resulting toward the end of the nineteenth century in a strong tendency toward individualism and a living for oneself. In the person of man evolution seemed to be acting like a jet of water approaching the top of its flight and breaking into single droplets. At the start of the twentieth century the isolation of human particles from one another and their need of autonomous activity had in fact reached a maximum, while the sense of community was almost entirely lost. In a very short time, however, all this changed and mankind now finds itself caught up in an accelerating movement toward what Teilhard calls " socialization ". The reason, he said, is that in our own time we have finally experienced the geographic saturation of the earth, which has in turn increased the psychic pressure of human life and changed the movement of man's history from one of expansion to one of contraction. This is what he calls the " rebound " of evolution, a fresh start for human energy towards " planetization " as well as toward a pole of convergence named Omega.

This mention of Omega as the goal of evolution underlines the overarching importance of the future for Teilhard both here and in another volume, *The Future of Man* (London and New York, Collins and Harper and Row, 1964), which should certainly be read after finishing *The Phenomenon*. " The past has revealed to me how the future is built." It is this preoccupation which is responsible for his extrapolation into the future of his law of complexity-consciousness, and the character of prophecy which this has given to much of his writing. Such extrapolation in turn led him to insist that the universe as he describes it in evolution depends ultimately upon the existence of a divine, personal Omega, who is alone capable of drawing human persons to himself by activating the love energy of the world. For in Teilhard's system the free circulation of love energy between persons is the only force which can unite mankind in true freedom, and for such love to be fostered it is first necessary that men believe that Omega is a present reality, " loving and lovable at this very moment ". Teilhard's description of the " Christian phenomenon " at the end of *The Phenomenon of Man* and in much of *The Future of Man* thus becomes the link between what he wrote for believers and what he wrote for those to whom he wished to bring the Christian message.

We may bring this Preface to a close by briefly noting four less important books by Teilhard in English, as well as three critical studies which may be helpful for those wishing to pursue his thought further. *Letters from a Traveller* (London and New York, Collins and Harper and Row, 1962), is a selection from the correspondence he had, mostly with relatives, during his frequent absences from France between 1923 and his death in 1955. Teilhard's comments on his experiences during these years make diverting reading, but they tell us relatively little about the development of his thought or even about his deepest feelings. Of much more value is the slim volume, *Correspondence* (New York, Herder and Herder, 1967), which brings together the theological exchange between Teilhard and Maurice Blondel in 1919. Two other collections of essays may also be of interest, *The Appearance of Man* and *The Vision of the Past* (London and New York, Collins and Harper and Row, 1965 and 1966), the former group dealing chiefly with the scientific aspects of human origins, the latter more concerned with the significance of these origins for man's present development. Many of these essays, written over a thirty-year period, are now dated scientifically, but they will all be of value to someone concerned with a further expansion of the early part of *The Phenomenon of Man*.

Finally we may recommend three evaluations in depth of Teilhard's vision of the universe. Henri de Lubac has written the longest of these, *The Religion of Teilhard de Chardin* (London and New York, Collins and Desclée, 1967). With the erudition characteristic of all his work, de Lubac studies the various elements in Teilhard's system from the viewpoint of his spiritual teaching, and makes a special effort to defend him against the charge of being unorthodox in his Christianity. Unlike de Lubac, whose presentation of ideas follows his own order rather than Teilhard's, the volume by Piet Smulders, *The Design of Teilhard de Chardin* (Westminster, Newman, 1967), and my own *Teilhard de Chardin and the Mystery of Christ* (London and New York, Collins and Harper and Row, 1966) make a point of keeping Teilhard's own scheme of development. The former scrutinizes the theological implications of Teilhard's evolutionary system, while the latter seeks to organize the whole of Teilhard's theological thought into a synthesis which he himself outlined a number of times but never actually made. The last mentioned work also contains a fairly representative bibliography of the more important articles which treat specialized topics of a scientific, philosophical or theological nature.

AUTHOR'S INTRODUCTION

"Science suggested a cosmology; and whatever suggests a cosmology suggests a religion." Alfred North Whitehead, *Religion in the making.*

One's first inclination is to regard Teilhard de Chardin's work as exhibiting a considerable degree of diversity. More than that, even—it makes an impression almost of chaos. A glance through his extensive bibliography is enough to establish at once how variegated was the sweep of his intellectual concern. He was an outstanding scientist in the fields of geology and palaeontology and wrote a large number of authoritative studies on those problematical subjects. Besides that, he developed—on the basis of insights and results attained by modern science—a kind of synthesis or phenomenology of the universe, considered as a phenomenon. He also wrote a lengthy succession of essays and articles in which he broached many problems in philosophy, theology and the history of culture.

When we take a more careful look, however, it soon becomes evident that all this many-sided and seemingly chaotic activity has in no small measure an inner, organic unity, so that it can be wholly reduced to a few central ideas, or, it might even be said, to one central problem. If on an outside view, so to speak, his work seems at times to be something of a hodge-podge, without any order, inwardly the whole is governed by one fundamental concern and by a single problem, personally experienced. This core of his mental life could be reduced to these two concepts: God and the universe. They form the twin poles of his thinking; and his whole endeavour was to be concentrated on the task of discovering the connection between them. Just as for a St. Augustine or a Cardinal Newman the core of all their thought and all their ideas is expressed in a pair of terms—*Deus et anima*, I and my Creator—so in the case of Teilhard de Chardin the whole interior attention of the

21

man centres upon the problem of the relation between God and the world.

On countless occasions he referred in his writings to the contrariety and inner tension which these two ideas had evoked in him. By temperament and occupation he knew himself to be " a child of earth ", attracted and uplifted by the spectacle of the cosmos to which he felt himself personally linked and the laws and structure of which, in their deeper operation, he strove to comprehend. By upbringing and intellectual training, however, he felt himself to be " a child of heaven ", nurtured upon and held by the profoundest and most powerful influences of the Christian religion. He knew from direct experience the teachings, the language and the " ethos " of both worlds.[1] We have his own word for the fact that the growth of his inner life and the conflicts that arose within it were entirely bound up with this perpetual confrontation between Heaven and Earth.[2]

For many people the world of science and the world of faith have nothing in common. They constitute two totally different territories, fenced off from each other by an impenetrable barrier. To begin with, this was also the case for Teilhard; but with this state of inner division, this intellectual and spiritual " schizophrenia ",[3] he found no contentment. His mind hankered after unity. He was impelled by an " insatiable need for cosmic organicity ".[4] This urge to unity, cohesion, synthesis, is one of the most characteristic properties of his mind. It is the " totality " that he wishes to encompass, and not just a constituent part or aspect of it. His experience is wholly governed, therefore, by the tension within him between what he calls " cosmic sense " and " Christic sense ". By cosmic sense or cosmic awareness he means the " more or less cosmic affinity that binds *us psychologically* with the All which encircles us ".[5] Christic sense or Christ-consciousness means for him the conviction on the part of Christians that Christ constitutes the centre and the final goal of all things.

At first—as he himself attests—he felt inwardly torn apart by the simultaneous presence in his heart and mind of this cosmic consciousness and this Christ-consciousness[6]. Between these two worlds he could descry no cohesion, no identity, until at last the synthesis which he so fervently aspired after was attained. As the years went by—and after much un-remitting strain and effort on his part—the cosmic and the Christic consciousness, which initially had arisen in his mind in total independence of each other, came to disclose their cohesion, convergence and fundamental unity.[7] This had nothing to do with some vague relationship between Christ and the world of matter, but involved the recognition that Christ had a cosmic function and that the evolution of the cosmos had to be seen as a movement orientated upon a cosmic central point.[8]

How all this is to be envisaged we shall see later on. For the time being we must pause momentarily to consider the question of what solutions are proposed to the problem, or—if you will—the dilemma, raised by the terms "God" and "the world".

Theoretically speaking, there are three possible approaches to dealing with this problem. One can scrap the term "God" and accept that the world is the only reality; or one can eliminate the term "world" and see only God as having a claim to be considered real; or one can retain both concepts and try to determine the proper connection between them.

The atheist will scratch the first term of the dilemma. He denies God's existence so as to be able to devote himself the more completely to the world and to his role within it. The concept of God is taken to be an obstacle to realizing the proper being of man. By thinking about God man forgets the demands of his life here on earth, or else he looks for an alibi in God, an excuse for his own inertia and resignation. In that way man becomes estranged from his own potentialities and his proper task in the world. This critical view has already been voiced by Hegel. "Our religion," he wrote in his juvenilia, "is intended to educate men as citizens of heaven, with their gaze fastened always upon the things above; and the result is that they grow strange toward all human sentiments and feelings";[9] and again: "The Christian is passive toward his God

and indifferent to the things of this world ".[10] This idea turns
up again in the present-day Marxist as well as among the
atheistic existentialists.

The second solution, diametrically opposite to the first,
consists in abandoning the concept " world ". For some mys-
tics in Hinduism, Buddhism and Islam the world is virtually
non-existent. Either they designate existence *per se* as a
nullity, so that the things of this world do not merit our
attention, or they are turned toward God to such a degree that
the world falls away, as it were, into nothingness. The world
is not infrequently described as an " appearance " and a
delusion, a transient and idle vanity, with which we should concern ourselves as little as possible. Among Christian writers too
this notion is sometimes to be found. Everything that is not
God—we read in the *Imitation*—is nothing, and as nothing is
to be despised.

In the third answer both concepts are maintained in full;
and our endeavour must be to discover a harmonious relation
between them. For Teilhard de Chardin this is the only direction in which the proper solution may be found. He invariably
allows their full weight to both the terms in question; and both
for him conserve their full reality. There was a period in his
life when pantheism did perhaps exercise a power of attraction
over his thinking; but that period was decidedly brief and
quickly made way for the unconditional affirmation of a personal God. The real problem of his life was therefore that of
the relationship between the personal God of Christianity and
the universe, the more profound nature of which modern
science is beginning to disclose to us.

This is not yet, however, an adequate account of the conflict within the man. The problem of God's relation to the
world—and vice versa—is first and foremost a metaphysical
one—and for the Christian a theological question too. But the
metaphysico-theological aspects of the problem were considered
by Teilhard as having for the most part been resolved. His
problem is not metaphysical in character at all; and only

occasionally does he touch upon what are really metaphysical questions. His true problem lies rather in the plane of living and of " lived religion " or, better, in the plane of action. The question that preoccupies him is how *love* for God and *love* of the world may be reconciled and brought into unity. His aim is to discover "how . . . we can reconcile, and provide mutual nourishment for, the love of God and the healthy love of the world, a striving towards detachment and a striving towards the enrichment of our human lives. . . , ".[11]

One cannot but be struck by the frequency with which such words come from his pen. At the very start of his scientific career he is found expressing the conviction that " a reconciliation must be possible between cosmic love of the world and heavenly love of God . . . between the cult of progress and the passion for the glory of God."[12]

His true concern and the very core of his thinking are expressed in those words. Strictly speaking, his was a practical problem, and not a metaphysical one at all.

What he was determined to do was to discover the unity in our actions, our aspirations and our work, to find an orientation for our activity that would be focussed at once upon God and the world. " Somewhere," he writes, " there must be a standpoint from which Christ and the earth can be so situated in relation to one another that it is impossible for me to possess the one without embracing the other, to be in communion with the one without being absorbed into the other, to be absolutely Christian without being desperately human ".[13]

These words may fairly be regarded as the major *Leitmotiv* that would continue to govern all his thinking from beginning to end. Only in the perspective of this fundamental concern can his work be properly understood and interpreted. Here lies the key to the secret of his mind's adventure. His whole endeavour is expressed in these words : " to elucidate the relationship through which the Kingdom of God and the exertions of mankind are genetically linked with each other."[14]

The noblest triumph, therefore, and the most precious con-

quest that he achieved in his life was—as he saw it—his discovery of "the marvellous and liberating harmony between a
religion of the Christic type and an Evolution of the convergent
type ".[15] "The major event of my life has been the gradual
identification on the horizon of my soul of two sources of
illumination, the first being the point of cosmic culmination
postulated by a universal process of evolution of a convergent
type and the other formed by the risen Christ of the
Christian faith ".[16]

Without a doubt, therefore, the problem of the relation
between God and the universe is central to all Teilhard de
Chardin's conceptualizing; and only on that basis is it
possible to grasp the unity and coherence of his very extensive
output. From this initial problem spring all the major themes
handled by him in his writings.

That is not all, however; for this problem of the relationship between God and the world was to his mind much more
than a purely abstract and theoretical question, suitable for
calm discussion at academic get-togethers or in dry-as-dust
treatises. For him this was a genuinely existential question
in which his whole being was implicated—as though his
existence as a human being and a Christian were here at stake.
The solution that he proposed is consequently more the outcome of a personal encounter with life, of a subjective experience, than of a purely scientific enquiry. What is involved for
him is in the first place a personal adventure—but one of
which the outcome, as he saw it, could well be of benefit to
others. It is noticeable how often he referred to the personal
and subjective character of this mental experience of his; and
it is perhaps only a slight exaggeration to say that on this
score he wanted to be not so much the teacher as the
testifier. When in his very last essay, *Le Christique* (1955)
he wants to propound yet again his Christo-cosmic conception
of the world, he speaks expressly of "bearing witness to a
certain personal experience" and in his autobiographical essay,

Le Coeur de la Matière (1950), his intention is "to give an account of a psychological experience to which I have been directly subjected—one which I have personally undergone and which was just sufficiently reflective to become intelligible and communicable, without losing its indisputably objective value". And a bit further on we read : "To Christify matter . . . therein lies the whole adventure of my inner life . . . A great and magnificent adventure". Time and again he utters sentiments of a similar kind whenever he comes to deal with this central problem of his life.

This accent on personal experience explains not only the none too orderly succession of his articles and essays, in which he very often returns to the same problems and indulges in a good deal of repetition, but also the extremely personal and moving, frequently poetic, form in which he casts his experiences and insights. This comes out more especially in the terminology he employs, which is a very marked departure from the technical language ordinarily used in philosophical and theological discourse. Everybody's thinking and way of expressing himself are conditioned, of course, by the mental climate in which he lives and moves. That is something which affects both the orientation of his thinking and the language that he brings to the expression of his ideas. The "mental climate" of Teilhard de Chardin was that of the natural sciences, of geology and palaeontology. He experienced it intensely and passionately; and it formed the context within which he reflected upon the great issues claiming his attention. The categories, concepts and terms which he was to employ in this reflective activity bear the stamp, therefore, of the natural sciences, of the milieu in which he was at home.

Not a few have seen fit to criticize him for that. When one is dealing with theological issues, they say, one should not only adopt a purely theological standpoint and observe the method proper to that discipline but also respect the terms and thought-categories established by age-old tradition and adapted to the subtlety of the matter in hand. This rebuke would be fair enough, no doubt, had Teilhard de Chardin really intended to play the part of a professional theologian. It is indeed true that neither the method of theology nor the accepted theological terminology figures in most of his writings as one might expect them to do. But Teilhard de Chardin never aspired to being recognized as a theologian. He declared most emphatically on many occasions that he did not regard himself as having any special theological competence. If any misunderstanding has arisen on this point, then he has certainly not been the cause of it. He wanted to be a man of science—but a scientist who was at the same time a man of faith, someone who did not keep his faith and his science in separate compartments but from an inner necessity strove for a harmonious synthesis between the two. He wanted to bear testimony to this inward experience, to the difficulties which he encountered in connection with it as well as to the results at which he was able to arrive. It is as the testimony of a great scientist and a great Christian, therefore, that his considered thoughts and ideas deserve our special attention.

That this kind of attestation can be fruitful in its results not only for the psychology of religion but for theological thinking too scarcely needs saying. Teilhard de Chardin knew very well that the circumstances in which life had placed him had allowed him to feel the full force of a number of difficulties in the relationship between the modern world and Christianity, more than is the case with most theologians; and by pointing to the problems which contemporary science and the mental outlook of modern man can yield for Christianity he has undoubtedly done something of real usefulness. From now on, the theologians cannot disregard these facts. Teilhard's work can only enrich theology and enable it to make significant advances, provided the theologians take notice of these experiences and probe more deeply into the solutions which he proposed.

On the other hand, the fact that Teilhard de Chardin often clothed his religious reflections in words and concepts taken from the natural sciences, although not without its dangers, has unmistakable advantages too. It simply is a fact that for contemporary man the language of theology presents very great difficulties, indeed has in many instances become quite unintelligible. Most of its accepted terms and forms of expression came into being under the influence of a philosophy with which scarcely anyone outside the Church is still conversant. Conserving these language forms has unquestionable advantages; but it carries the drawback of making access to the world of theological ideas extremely hard for modern man. The fact is that in transposing Catholic doctrine into terms borrowed from modern science Teilhard de Chardin made access to Christianity easier for a lot of people and succeeded in arousing renewed interest in many religious values long forgotten.

In this connection it is perhaps a good thing to recall for a moment some words spoken by John XXIII in his opening address to the Second Vatican Council, when he referred to the need " to make a distinction between the substance of the faith and the formulas in which during the course of time it has come to be expressed "—words which make crystal clear the relative character of theological formulas and turns of phrase and invite us to search for forms in which to express the truth of the faith in the spirit of our times.

Now it is true that Teilhard de Chardin often omitted to draw in sharp lines and to delimit the concepts with which he operated, and true also that this not infrequently gave rise to a degree of vagueness—not to say of ambiguity. That his work needs further completion in this respect nobody will deny. Yet perhaps one could also say about him what Professor R. C. Kwant has said of the philosopher Merleau-Ponty: " He acquired an original outlook on reality; and such an outlook searches after new concepts and in any case gives new significance to the old ones. It is characteristic of new concepts that they arise as and when they are needed for use, that they are worked with before they are defined by reflection . . . He is a thinker who in the very act of composition is still searching after truth; and some of his concepts are brought to birth, as it were, during composition. We have to respect this character of his work and so take care not to attribute to him any completed, definitive and sharply demarcated concepts."[17]

The criticism that has been voiced regarding Teilhard de Chardin's terminology must therefore be reduced to its proper proportions. Had it been his purpose to play the professional theologian, then one might indeed find a deal of fault with his writings; but when we allow for the fact that his religious writings are to be seen as first and foremost the testimony to a highly personal experience, these strictures—in our view—lose most of their force. If he had been obliged to use a different method and a different language, not only would the authenticity of his witness have been put under a severe strain, but it would then be completely unintelligible to most of our contemporaries.

To speak precisely, one might perhaps say that the paradox of Teilhard de Chardin consists in the fact that he makes the world of the natural sciences his starting-point for the solution of a religious and theological problem. Therein lies his originality and his real merit. It was good that someone of his distinction should commit himself to so risk an undertaking and should commuincate the outcome to his fellow men. Others in their turn will be able to test the results of his spiritual adventures by their own experiences and subject them, where necessary, to deeper investigation.

If Teilhard de Chardin was determined to express this adventure of his own mind and spirit with so much devotion and so much attention to detail, the justification for that is not far to seek; nor indeed is it difficult to explain. He was profoundly convinced that his problem was one of the most important confronting man at the present time, and hence that any results he had attained could be of use and benefit to others.

The problem that he experienced with such intensity is, in the end, simply that of the encounter between the modern world—wholly dominated as it is by science—and Christianity.

That, to a very large extent, is the problem facing every thoughtful Christian. Consciously or unconsciously, we all experience the tension that exists between the two worlds and underlies the crisis in our Western culture. The result of this conflict often is that some are wholly engrossed by a this-worldly culture and its values, rejecting all religions as forms of self-alienation, while others incarcerate themselves within an other-worldly Christianity and give no thought to the world's values at all. To build a synthesis of the positive values enshrined within modern culture and the imperishable substance of the Christian revelation is thus one of the most pressing tasks for Christian thinking in our time. " The new world of to-day ", says the theologian M. D. Chenu, " has certainly not as yet been integrated into Christian thought . . . I am convinced that in full loyalty to the message of the Gospel we are going to construct a rational confrontation with the world, an outlook on the world in which there will continue to be room for different tendencies within the fundamental unity of the Gospel. It is an onerous task; but it would indeed be a sad thing if the urge to renewal which is making its influence felt in so many areas of the Church's life were to be brought to a standstill by our unwillingness to frame a rational system vis-à-vis the world's problems ".[18]

It could hardly be better put. But then it at once becomes apparent how much Teilhard de Chardin's endeavour is completely in line with the present striving within the Christian fold. In fact, Père Chenu admits as much in so many words : " It has often been my experience, among an enormous variety of people, including some of the working class, to hear them talk about and discuss Teilhard de Chardin as though it were a quite natural and obvious thing to do and as though here were an author who is a kindred spirit. I have the impression that the ideas for which Teilhard de Chardin was able to provide a scientific substructure answer to a very widespread state of mind and very widespread yearnings ".[19]

Thus the problem which it was Teilhard de Chardin's lot to encounter is one that sooner or later confronts every thoughtful

Christian. His experience is not to be taken as something quite out of the ordinary run but ought rather to be seen as exemplifying how countless Christians are searching and thinking. It is not really astonishing, therefore, that his writings have met with such a big response in the world of today. Contemporary men find themselves addressed and stirred, more even by his broadly human and religious message than by his purely scientific insights. " If so many people have felt that Teilhard de Chardin was speaking to them, perhaps that is to be explained primarily by the fact that he succeeded in re-making a temple of the universe."[20] A spirituality which takes no account of mundane values has become insupportable to modern man. Gabriel Marcel echoes the opinion of many : " It is my deepest and most unshakable conviction ", he wrote, "—and if it is heretical, so much that the worse for orthodoxy —that whatever all the thinkers and doctors have said, it is not God's will at all to be loved by us as *against* the creation, but rather glorified by us *through* the creation and with the creation as our starting point. That is why I find so many religious works intolerable. A god who opposes himself to what he has created and is envious, as it were, of his own handiwork, is in my eyes a false god and nothing more ".[61]

Since this is indeed the state of men's minds, an experience like that of Teilhard de Chardin is nothing exceptional; but from that it follows that what he was seeking to attest deserves our particular attention and is of outstanding importance for the intellectual and spiritual life of our times. That is why he merits our esteem, not only as a fine scientist and a distinguished Christian but still more as an extraordinary witness to what is now taking place in the recesses of the human soul.

It is a curious thing that Teilhard de Chardin arouses admiration and enthusiasm in some people, whereas others are just as decidedly hostile and ready to dismiss him. Whence these conflicting reactions? Are the former less critical and more gullible, the latter more stringent in applying their scientific, philosophical or theological standards? It is not at all easy to make out a case along those lines. In both camps—among his admirers as well as his opponents—there are people who take very seriously indeed the standards demanded by science and by philosophical and theological reflection. We believe, therefore, that for an explanation of this one has to look elsewhere. In most instances—or so it would seem to us—a person's reaction to Teilhard de Chardin's work is largely determined by the inner experience of the individual concerned.

If a man has experienced for himself the problem of the tension between modern culture and Christianity (or, in general, belief in God), between admiration for what science and technics have created and the ideals of the Gospel, between hopes centred on this world and hopes centred on the next, "between the cult of progress and the passion for the glory of God", then he will feel himself almost instinctively drawn to Teilhard de Chardin, will recognize in him a fellow-traveller and will meet in his writings a wealth of insights that can prove of major importance in helping to resolve his inner conflict. For many people of this sort becoming acquainted with the whole world of his ideas has proved to be a kind of intellectual and spiritual deliverance for which they will always be grateful.

If, however, a man has never undergone this inner tension and feels firmly ensconced in some ideology or other or in some more traditional train of ideas, he will see Teilhard as a kind of disruptive influence and will make a special point of highlighting this or that methodological or philosophical shortcoming and so of concerning himself more with secondary points of detail than with the considerably inspired character of the whole. Thus Teilhard turns out to be the effective centre and cause of a division of minds, which can often be traced more to a quality of inward experience than to any external and objective criteria.

In the meantime it is good that the debate should continue on both sides. Blind admiration might simply mean—in total contradiction of Teilhard's own intentions—that one was

happy to accept the results already achieved and to let it go
at that; whilst the effect of a too one-sidedly critical view
must be to make one forget or overlook the really valuable
insights contained in his writings. The main thing is that his
spiritual experience should be of service to others and should
continue to act as a leaven upon the intellectual life of
Christianity and of mankind.

PART I

An Evolution with a Convergent Character

Chapter 1

TOWARDS A SCIENTIFIC PHENOMENOLOGY OF THE UNIVERSE

It was the opinion of St. Thomas Aquinas—in which he concurred with Aristotle—that the highest ideal of man the thinker must be to reflect, right up to its final causes, the whole world order—*totus ordo universi*—in his mind and spirit.[1] That was the highest perfection to which our intellect ought to aspire. Such an endeavour was in Aquinas' day entirely comprehensible; for the fact is that men in general were convinced that in its structure and composition the universe was, or could be, known with sufficient certainty. The Greeks had drawn up an inventory of the world and had described the general make-up of the cosmos. It did not occur to anyone to doubt the rightness of their doctrine. The earth formed the centre of the universe. Around the earth there were a number of concentric spheres (sun, moon and the five planets known at that time), by which it was completely encircled; and around all this there was an eighth sphere containing the fixed stars (the *fixae*). Upon earth there lived the plants and animals, placed at man's service, providing him with food and clothing and also assisting him in innumerable ways in his battle with ills and dangers of every kind.

Thus heaven and earth constituted a beautifully ordered whole, within which all things had their place and purpose— a whole that bore witness to the wisdom and omnipotence of the Creator and allowed man to find a meaningful place for himself within the great totality of things. Everything was made for man, was centred upon him and took from him its

37

meaning and its *raison d'être*. Such was the picture of the
world that formed the backcloth to medieval thought in its
every aspect; and no one can hope rightly to understand and
assess medieval philosophy and theology at their proper
worth who fails to reckon with this cosmological background.
That was the setting in which they envisaged man; and it was
within that kind of a world that they pondered upon God and
revelation. It lies as much at the back of Dante's *Divina
Commedia* as of Thomas's *Summa Theologica*. Their anthro-
pology and their theology flowed from their cosmology. The
existence of an undisputed, universally received picture of the
world—conceived as a perfect order in which everything occupied a meaningful place—gave to their thinking its coherent
and balanced character.

But the discoveries of Copernicus and Galileo put an end
to this way of picturing the world. In 1543, a few weeks
before his death, Copernicus published his *De Revolutionibus
Orbium Caelestium*, in which he showed that the old geo-
centrism was untenable. To begin with, his ideas met with
only a limited response; but when Galileo appeared, they did
get through to the public at large. From then on men began
to realize that the framework, the view of the world with
which they had felt at home for centuries past, had suddenly
ceased to exist. At about the same time another world-shaking
discovery was made. The Dutchman, Anthony van Leeuwen,
constructed the first microscope; and all at once a whole new
world of the minutest creatures came to light for the first
time. It is still hard for us to realize what commotion and
confusion all this brought in its train. To little or no purpose
men began to wonder in what mysterious and incomprehensible
world it was that they now found themselves and what their
place might still be in such a cosmos. Did it indeed still
make sense to speak of a "cosmos", now that everything had
begun to look so confused and incoherent? This feeling of
uncertainty is to go on increasing all the time, as science makes
fresh advances and discloses ever new aspects of reality, quite
unsuspected before.

Since the Graeco-Arabian world view disintegrated, men have never really succeeded in forming a coherent picture of the universe, in which they might find a place and meaning for their existence. Some indeed simply closed their eyes to the new situation and behaved as though nothing had happened. Others, however, tended more and more to recognize our powerlessness to see the cosmos as a meaningful whole and to allot man his place in so incoherent a world. What was man, if not a totally accidental and superfluous by-product in some remote corner or other of an impenetrable and absurd universe? The result was that philosophical reflection increasingly forsook the contemplation of nature, withdrawing wholly within the frontiers of human subjectivity and human history. Descartes' "*cogito*" became the point of departure for numerous philosophies whose sole concern was with the subject; whilst Immanuel Kant went further and saw the idea of a "cosmos" as charged with an intrinsic antinomy which set it once for all beyond the reach of the human mind. Thus the whole of philosophy was reduced, step by step, to analysis of the human *modus existendi,* approached and assessed exclusively in terms of the subject's experience of being.

In the most recent period such great advances have been made in the field of the natural sciences that some people have once more begun to ask themselves whether we are not on the road to forming a new and coherent view of the totality of things, as a result of which man may again find it possible to discover his own place—and to do so in a way which makes sense and is scientifically warranted. Many scientists to-day have a feeling that the various natural sciences, which until now have been so carefully distinguished and kept separate from one another, are tending more and more to converge; so that the boundaries between astronomy, physics, chemistry and biology are becoming increasingly vague and the world is beginning to appear to us once again as a fundamental unity. The discovery of the principle of evolution, the contribution made by a man like Albert Einstein, the construction of the giant telescope at Mount Palomar and so many other great

events in the area of the natural sciences have given us a new
vision of the cosmos, with the result that at any rate in its
main features a new image of the world is beginning to take
shape—and already we begin to hear some talk of a "third
cosmology". After the world view presented by Graeco-
Arabian science, after the fragmentary cosmologies which followed in the wake of Galileo, a new period would now seem
to be dawning in which it will be possible for man to discover
his place and function in the world as a whole. "Our age,"
wrote Sir Julian Huxley, " is the first in which we can obtain a
picture of man's place and role in nature which is both reasonably comprehensive and based on scientific knowledge. We
can be sure that the picture is still very imperfect, that its
comprehensiveness will be much enlarged, and that its scientific basis will be powerfully strengthened; but the fact remains that our century is the first in which any both comprehensive and scientific picture has become possible."[2]

Among the scientists who have given themselves to this
task the French Jesuit, Pierre Teilhard de Chardin, has a very
special place. Not only did he attempt—on the basis of his
copious experience and wealth of information as a scientist—
to construct in outline a coherent notion of the cosmos and,
above all, of the place of man within this universe, but he also
drew attention to the philosophical and theological consequences which, as he believed, are implied in this new vision
of the world. His ideas have aroused not only tremendous
admiration but some keen opposition too. At any rate they
are worth examining with care. Even though his work may
only be regarded as a first attempt, a reconnaissance in the
direction that we have indicated, still the impulses emanating
from his ideas at this present moment are considerable enough
to justify our taking the trouble to acquaint ourselves with
his opinions and to pursue the question of whether his ideas
really do have a sound basis or not. In committing his work
to writing that was all that he himself ever had in mind.

i *Teilhard's Scientific Career*

Pierre Teilhard de Chardin was born on 1 May 1881, on the family estate at Sarcenat near Orcines (about seven kilometres west of Clermont-Ferrand in the Auvergne). His mother was a great-grandniece of Voltaire. Teilhard was the fourth in a family of eleven children, many of whom, however, were to die at an early age. After completing his secondary education at the Collège Notre-Dame at Mongré (Villefranche-sur-Saône), at the age of eighteen he joined the Society of Jesus. It was quite early on, during his formative years at the house of study in Jersey and his brief spell of teaching physics at the Jesuit College in Cairo (1906-8), that he started to take a special interest in geological and palaeontological questions. He was to qualify himself further in those subjects at the University of Paris where, after an interruption of his studies occasioned by the War, he proceeded in 1922 to a doctorate in the natural sciences. Especially important for his later work were the classes held by Professor Marcellin Boule, who initiated him into the field of human palaeontology and was to remain a lifelong friend.

Meanwhile he had already obtained a lectureship in geology at the Institut Catholique in Paris; but this was not to last for very long. In 1923 he was sent on a scientific mission to China; and for more than twenty years Asia was to captivate him and claim his attention as a scientist. He took an active part in numerous scientific expeditions which made a call upon his geological and palaeontological expertise. In his expert capacity he was associated with the Roy Chapman Andrews expedition of the American Museum of Natural History (1930), with the Haardt-Citroën expedition (1931-2), the Yale-Cambridge expedition to North and Central India (1935-8) and the Harvard-Carnegie expedition in Burma (1937-8). Previous to this he had been nominated adviser to the Geo-

logical Survey of China and had even completed a couple or
so of missions to French Somaliland and the Harar (1928-9).
All these travels and investigations " in the field" were
extraordinarily rich in valuable discoveries that earned him
an enduring reputation as a scientist and lent him considerable
authority among his professional colleagues.

After the Second World War he went home and was appointed Director of the research office of the Centre National
de la Recherche Scientifique in Paris. He was also offered a
Chair at the Collège de France; but he spent the last years of
his life in New York, where in 1951 he was made permanent
assistant at the Wenner-Gren Foundation for Anthropological
Research. His work for this institution took him twice to
South Africa (1951 and 1953), where his task was to stimulate and improve the co-ordination of systematic enquiry in the
field of human prehistory. Furthermore, he was an Honorary
Fellow of the Royal Anthropological Institute of Great Britain
and Ireland, a member of the French Academy of Sciences, an
honorary member of the Academy of Sciences of New York
and a member of the American Association for Geology. He
died in New York on Easter Day, 10 April 1955.

Even this bare summary gives one some intimation of what
an active part he played in the scientific life of his time. What
with excavations and journeys of exploration and the labora-
tory work which these entailed, the industry he displayed was
indeed enormous; and through it he succeeded in enriching
very considerably our knowledge of the past in a variety of
fields. Then again, the example which he set—and his engaging personality—has been of great influence in providing a
stimulus to a lot of youthful energy and an incitement to
further study and research.

Teilhard was a scientific investigator of real stature. Within
the area of his special field of knowledge he has left behind
him some very important work of undisputed weight and validity. The long list of his technical contributions, reports and
communications is to be found in the bibliography compiled
by Claude Cuénot : it amounts to nearly forty compact pages.[3]

His pure research was chiefly concerned with three areas. To begin with, in the sphere of pure geology he broke new ground with his researches into the structure and physiography of the soil of China. Here he succeeded in completing a double geological section, one in an east-west direction, running from Shantung to the Pamir, the second from north to south, from Manchuria (Harbin) to the borders of Indo-China, through territories still largely unexplored by science at that time. This operation brought to light a great deal of evidence about the geological structure of East Asia.

And then in the area of mammal palaeontology. His studies in this field had to do with the fauna of the early tertiary in France, Belgium and England; but his main discoveries relate to the fossil mammals of North China. His chief claim to distinction as a palaeontologist, though, is in the field of human prehistory. What lay at the centre of his concern and drew his interest the most was man himself—his origins and his history. He gave himself with tremendous application to the study of those scanty traces that the soil has preserved of the earlier races of men. He personally visited many of the sites where human fossils have been discovered, so that he would be in a better position to assess the worth of the skeletal fragments found at these places. Sometimes he was personally involved in making the discovery. Thus his name—along with those of Davidson Black, W. C. Pei and F. Weidenreich—will always be associated with one of the most important finds in the field of human palaeontology : the discovery of *Sinanthropus pekinensis*, made between 1929 and 1937 at Chou-Kou-Tien, about fifty kilometres south-west of Pekin.

Teilhard possessed to an outstanding degree the temperament for scientific enquiry : an indefatigable worker, extremely exact in his methods of research and observation, always receptive to any fresh insight, he rendered—and this is the view of his scientific colleagues generally—very great services to science. His scientific work—so Professor J. Piveteau has written—" has opened up wide and noble perspectives; it has given us a new outlook on the world; it has set his stamp

on one of the major stages in the development of palaeontology."[4]

We particularly wanted to dwell for a moment here on Teilhard's merits as a scientist, because they show the extent to
which the world view that he evolved was firmly grounded in a
thorough acquaintance with the facts which science now has
at its disposal and which form the solid infrastructure of his
understanding of the world. The synthesis which he proposed
was not the work of a dilettante or a dreamer but of a man
who had applied himself throughout a lifetime meticulously
to the study of natural phenomena and had acquired a considerable mastery in his chosen field. He was in the first
instance a geologist and palaeontologist—and not a philosopher or theologian. His intellectual orientation was that of
the student of nature; and this was his commanding interest.
It came before all the rest of his work and forms as it were an
extension of it.

ii " *To comprehend the universe* "

The data which biology and geology had yielded regarding the
history of the earth and of life were for Teilhard an inexhaustible store of matter for further and more comprehensive reflection. Besides a long succession of purely scientific studies,
therefore, he also wrote a great number of essays and articles
in which he described, from a changing standpoint, that vision
of the world which was maturing in his mind out of the daily
contact he had with contemporary science. These writings of
his were not, as a rule, at all systematic. They were written
on the spur of the moment—now because some fresh insight
had occurred to him or because he wanted to clarify and probe
more deeply into a theme which he had already taken up on
some earlier occasion, now again in order to meet the wishes
of a friend or to provide a contribution to some periodical or
other, when requested by the editor to do so. On first acquaintance these writings make a somewhat chaotic impression; but

when one examines them more closely, one can see that they were all born of an identical inspiration and in their general tenor form a balanced and harmonious whole. We must not forget that their author was a man almost continuously on the move, that he seldom had a library available and did not even have at his elbow what he had written on previous occasions. That is why he often repeated himself in these essays and why in point of form they do not present a rounded and finished whole. We ought rather to understand them as a prolonged series of attempts to express more purely and perfectly the stupendous and inexhaustible subject on which they were written. Most of the essays were not published till after the author's death; and a good part of them remain unpublished even now. The matter has been taken in hand by the publishing house of Le Seuil in Paris; and publication is being sponsored by a broadly based committee which includes many of the world's front-rank scholars and scientists.

A new facet of Teilhard's copious mind is revealed in these essays. He was not only a scientist able to examine in a spirit of matter-of-factness and objectivity the smallest details and peculiarities of a fossil lower jaw or to trace with the utmost accuracy the structures of the earth's layers in a given region. He was a thinker too, all the time concerned to ponder the general human implications of the discoveries made and to bring together the multiplicity of insights thus obtained into a harmonious and scientifically warranted synthesis. With the same passion that he brought to the scrutiny of the terrestrial strata and to the examination of fossils down to the minutest detail he strove to construct an all-embracing picture of the world, in which each phenomenon would have its proper place and would disclose its precise significance for the whole. Thus there grew in him what he himself called: a desire for totality and completeness, a disposition of the mind to survey from an elevated standpoint the totality of things and to conceive the universe as a unity. For him analysis only made sense, in the last instance, in so far as it held to a synthesis in which everything could be reduced to its initial unity.

It is chiefly these essays that have served to draw the attention of a wider public to the name of Teilhard de Chardin. His strictly scientific studies have in the nature of things been more the reserve of specialists in geology and palaeontology; but the writings in which he devoloped his world view were addressed to a much wider public. It is in them that he deals with problems that are the concern of every thoughtful individual—problems for which he looks to find an answer. Especially in periods like our own, when nearly everyone has come to realize that the old notion of the world, with its limited dimensions and its mechanistic and static character, definitely belongs to the past and in face of the advances made by science a new way of conceiving how things are has come to take its place, it is understandable that many people should be on the look-out for a mentor able to guide them into this new world.

Not every man of science is in a position to do that. Either from natural inclination or for well defined reasons many confine themselves to the limited area of their special subject. That too is an attitude worthy of respect. Over-hasty generalizations and rashly constructed theories have done all too much harm at one time or another to the real progress of science. And again we must remember that not every science lends itself to being used as a point of departure for a synthesis which covers everything. In all scientific enquiry caution and a patient corroboration of the facts are always a prime necessity. Observation and experiment alone can form a basis for our knowledge of nature.

None of this, however, alters the fact that what the intellect desiderates is that our conception of the world should have both unity and coherence. Even for scientific progress it can be profitable to make the attempt from time to time to assemble the facts and to base a provisional synthesis upon them—one that in turn may prove a stimulus to new research and do splendid service as a " working hypothesis ". Thus we find that quite a number of scientists—and those not the least considerable—at the end of a long career wholly devoted to study and research have felt the need to draw together their

store of discoveries and the insights which they have acquired
into a general synthesis, and to project a world view arising
out of their reflections on these data.

Teilhard also felt such a need. He considered his interpretation of the world to be in some measure perhaps even the
finest and most original product of his scientific researches.
The depth of his insights and the grandeur of his vision make
this enterprise of his certainly one of the most remarkable of
our time.

Admittedly, such undertakings are always more or less
provisional in character and always capable of being improved
or supplemented in one way or another. So far as the main
lines and general orientation of his world view are concerned,
he certainly regarded these as definitive and as an acquisition
on the part of science; but further investigation would be
bound to fill out and improve the picture in many respects. It
is worthy of note, meanwhile, that as eminent a biologist as
Sir Julian Huxley, although an agnostic, has expressed his
great admiration and esteem for *The Phenomenon of Man*—
the work in which Teilhard has left us the most detailed
account of his vision of the world : " The force and purity of
Père Teilhard's thought and expression, in fruitful combination with his capacity for loving comprehension of all values,
has given the world a picture not only of rare clarity but
pregnant with compelling conclusions." He goes on to say
that, excepting certain points of detail, his personal reflection
had led him to the same conclusions : " The book as a whole
is outstanding . . . *Le Phénomène Humain* gives us a new and
vivifying vision of the process of reality."[5]

iii *A Phenomenology of the Universe*

The primary and major theme on which Teilhard deliberated
was the universe. What has it to teach us about its intrinsic
structure and development?

What too are man's place and man's task in this strange and

marvellous world? These are the questions to which he devoted himself with such intensive application throughout a lifetime. He sought an answer by way of the natural sciences and by constructing a scientific phenomenology.

It is possible to study man and the world from a great variety of standpoints. Thus one may try to interpret them from a metaphysical, theological or—where man is concerned—ethical standpoint. Each of these aspects constitutes the subject-matter of a different discipline. But the world can also be studied purely as a phenomenon, without any reference to the metaphysical, theological or ethical aspect : " Solely as a phenomenon, but also as the whole phenomenon."[6] This brings us very close to what the natural sciences are getting at; but they are confined each to this or that aspect of reality, and so are split up into innumerable specialist activities, each in its own field endeavouring through empirical observation and experiment to attain to deeper knowledge of the phenomenon under scrutiny. Each science severally gives us only a partial insight into the world phenomenon. That is why in systematizing the sciences we have to find a place for a study of the world taken *in toto*, without in so doing departing from whatever scheme the phenomena present. What we have in view here is the effort to comprehend the universe as that manifests itself to the observer—as " phenomenon ", and nothing more. An enterprise of this sort is called by Teilhard a phenomenology of the cosmic. Such a phenomenology, therefore, is a science which seeks to describe the universe as an observable phenomenon in its totality and its intrinsic cohesion, and to discover the meaning concealed in that totality.

We must not lose sight of the fact that the whole is more than the sum of its constituent parts. A plant is more than the sum of the chemical elements occurring in it. The world too is more than the sum of the entities found in it; and because that is so, it is not enough just to combine the results obtained from the various natural sciences in order to arrive at a true picture of what the world really is.

Within the total spectrum of the natural sciences—or at any rate in close association with them—a place must be found for a science which is concerned with the totality of the cosmic phenomenon and seeks to probe right into its structure and inner dynamic—assisted in this, of course, by everything that the other sciences have achieved in their several fields, but embracing and transcending all that, having regard to what is most specifically distinctive of the whole.

A proper analysis of the cosmic phenomenon necessarily goes further, therefore, than the results yielded by the subsidiary sciences; and that being so, it must have freedom of recourse to extrapolations and hypotheses. On the other hand, it has nothing to do with philosophy or, as the case may be, with metaphysics, which seeks to uncover the deeper principles and final causes of this world.

A true science of totality holds a kind of middle position between the various natural sciences on the one hand and philosophy proper on the other. To construct a science of this sort was precisely what Teilhard de Chardin aimed to do; and he defended over and over again the legitimacy of such an attempt, pointing out what its limits and methods are.[7]

We said just now that a science of this sort not only sets out to describe the world in its totality but also to uncover the inner meaning that lies concealed within the world phenomenon. The wish to comprehend the world in its totality as a phenomenon presupposes in the first place that we take fully into account the insights of modern science and take care to exclude every preconception in the course of assimilating the established facts. When we contemplate the world as a whole, we have no right to restrict our view to " primary experience ", so called, or to one part of scientific experience only, at the expense of those elements which for one non-scientific reason or another we find less to our liking. On the contrary, we are bound to exclude every apriority, thus allowing full weight to the total scientific experience and to all the available data, in the spirit in which science presents them to us.

But also part and parcel of such a phenomenology is the

study of the inner meaning of the world phenomenon. Indeed
the inner meaning of a phenomenon is an intrinsic aspect of it;
and so long as its significance escapes us, we cannot claim to
have understood the phenomenon itself. An example may
make this clearer. Take, for instance, a timepiece. We can
study this object under all its aspects : its dimensions, weight,
shape, make-up. We can investigate its constituent parts one
by one and in the smallest detail. But we can never say that
we have understood the timepiece *qua* timepiece, so long as
the purpose of this object has not dawned upon us, so long as
we do not know that in its totality and with all its subsidiary
parts it is *meant to do something*, namely, to indicate the hour
of the day, to measure time. It is reasonable, therefore, to
assert that we do not overstep the limits of the phenomenon
when we include in our investigation the end or purpose for
which it is actually intended, and that a true phenomenology
(in the sense stated) has not fully done its job so long as it
has failed to make clear to us what the meaning or purpose of
the phenomenon is. It goes without saying that what is here
referred to is the objective function of the phenomena, the purposiveness actually inherent in them, and not such purpose or
significance as may be imputed to them from outside.

Teilhard's phenomenology, then, may be characterized as
an endeavour, through the use of scientific expertise, to give
as complete as possible expression to the world in its totality
and inner orientation. It will be evident at once that what
he had in mind here should not be seen as a closed and definitive system. He was convinced that the way in which he saw
and represented the world corresponds to the current position
in science; but obviously it is, and will remain, open to being
supplemented and improved. Like every man of science,
Teilhard feels only distaste for a static and closed system, of
whatever sort. He is out to find the main lines on which it
may be possible to advance and deepen our knowledge of the
world and to lay bare its hidden structure.[8]

As to the rest, we may leave it to the philosopher and the
theologian to illuminate the world from their respective stand-

points. As soon as we start treading the ground of philosophy and theology, the task proper to physical science is done—and its writ ceases to run. This is not to say that the physical scientist must regard all consideration on his part of philosophical and theological issues as so much forbidden territory, but only that he must always be aware of making the transition and must allow for the fact that every branch of knowledge has its own method and internal rules of procedure.

To obviate any possible misunderstanding, it will not be beside the point here to offer a little clarification of the term "phenomenology". It has come very much into vogue in recent years, thanks primarily to Edmund Husserl; and it points us to one of the most important tendencies in modern philosophy. Phenomenology as Teilhard conceives of it has little in common with the kind pursued by Husserl and his disciples, although we may agree with d'Armagnac that between the two understandings of the term there is a measure of affinity.[9]

In its broadest and most general sense the term "phenomenology" signifies "a descriptive study of a whole set of phenomena".[10] Among contemporary philosophers, however, the term has acquired a restricted connotation. Their descriptive study is centred exclusively on the phenomena of consciousness and on the life of the mind : it invariably relates to the life of the psyche. With Teilhard, on the other hand, it is a matter of "the totality of the cosmic phenomenon",[11] which he aims to describe in terms of its structure and intrinsic meaning. Teilhard, says d'Armagnac, does for the process of being, in its totality, what the phenomenologists do in the sphere of psychology : he tries to read off and to distinguish the essential character of the phenomena through their development, to descry their nature through the course which they pursue from their origination to their final term.

If there is any link between Teilhard and the contemporary phenomenologists, it is to be looked for in the fact that for Teilhard too every effort to grasp the significance of the phenomena stands in a relation to man, seen not only in terms of his structure and his connection with other structures, but above all in his interiority. Whereas the contemporary phenomenologists incarcerate themselves, so to speak, in the study of the interiority, Teilhard's reflections merely bring him to the point of that interiority, without seeking to penetrate any further into it. The two forms of phenomenology differ where their object is concerned; but in the attitudes which they assume toward that object it is possible to discover a certain affinity.

We may try to elucidate this problem from yet another standpoint. In his *Existence et Signification* Professor A. de Waelhens includes a study of the relationship between science, phenomenology and ontology.[12] The phenomenology which Professor de Waelhens has in mind is, of course, that of contemporary philosophy. What difference, what distinction, then, does he envisage between science and that type of phenomenology?

To answer that question we have to consider for a moment the nature of the cognitive process in man. In the last analysis all knowing is an encounter of the knower with the object known, a state of " subsisting together ", a co-existing of the I with the other. This means that a twofold orientation is made possible. I can concentrate my attention wholly on the object and so make an abstraction, as it were, of my subjective state vis-à-vis this object. This is in fact the stance adopted by the scientist. Science is then—as Husserl has it—any systematic, " world-ly " knowing that comes about, *irrespective* of the act by which it does so. We leave out of the picture the subjective element present in all cognitive activity in order to take account solely of the object upon which that activity is focussed. The object is tendered to us, as it were : it is tendered to us as the *a priori* datum which we propose to assess as faithfully as we can in its objective givenness.

But we can also take a different approach. We can also fix our attention on the other element of knowing : namely, the subject in his cognitive activity. We can elect to investigate the nature not of the object perceived but of our perception itself, of the knowing subject in his many and various modalities and guises. It would then be the description of this "subjective" element of the perceptional encounter that would constitute the proper field of operation for phenomenology, the aim of which would be to analyse as clearly as possible the range of consciousness, in all the variety of its contents.

On this view, therefore, there is a clear and radical distinction to be made between science and phenomenology; but it will be evident at once that this idea of things will not do at all for phenomenology as Teilhard conceives it.

Strictly speaking—and with every allowance made for Professor de Waelhens' distinctions—Teilhardian phenomenology really lies somewhere between science and the phenomenology of Husserl, with the added proviso that it is much more closely related to the first than to the second. The truth is that with Teilhard it is the "object" that counts and that demands his whole attention, whilst the epistemological problems and psychological niceties of analysis lie pretty well entirely outside his purview.

From all this one would think it legitimate to conclude that where their design and purpose are concerned, Teilhard's phenomenology—based as it is on the natural sciences—and the psychological phenomenology of Husserl and his disciples differ totally from each other. The one point of contact detectable between them is that Teilhard's cosmic phenomenology leads ultimately to a very marked accentuation of "interiority", although without much attempt to examine this in its inner structure. That task must be the proper and exclusive field for psychological phenomenology.

iv *The Integral World View*

It will by now have become apparent that the phenomenology (or hyper-physics or *Weltanschauung*) which Teilhard aims at is nothing other than a way—as exact as he could make it—of describing the universe, abstracting every presentation

of a metaphysical or epistemological problem and so assimilating as much as possible to the data provided by the natural
sciences—on the understanding, of course, that the *de facto*
purposiveness, the inner orientation, the objective " meaning "
of the phenomenon being observed is integral to the enquiry.

The goal to which we aspire, therefore, is " to comprehend
the universe in its totality, in its inner cohesion, in its immàn-
ent meaning ". Yet " total world " is not merely the world
which exists as of *now*. We can never succeed in really understanding the world so long as we are obliged to restrict our
view to the present alone. Just as we cannot fully understand
a human individual if we make no allowance for the whole
course which his life has taken, so a complete knowledge of
the world must be conditional upon our having been able to
survey the entire course of universal evolution, from beginning
to end. To comprehend a motion it is not enough to isolate
from the curve a single moment and to study that by itself.
Really to know an individual—a Rubens, let us say, or a da
Vinci or a Pascal—we have to keep in view the whole of his
life and of his work; and of course it will not do to isolate a
random moment of his existence and found our judgment
solely on that. There is not a single existent having life or
motion that can be known, unless our consideration of it
allows full room for its historical dimension.[13]

All this has a bearing on the manner in which we envisage
the world. That the universe in which we live does not have a
static character but on the contrary has passed through a long
course of evolution cannot—and this we shall deal with in
more detail later on—in the light of modern science be any
longer open to doubt. It follows that when we pose the
problem of the world's meaning, we are really—when all is
said and done—asking about the meaning of a course of
events. To want to understand the world is to want to understand a process, a history. Just as an inert or apparently dead
man does not disclose to us what the full reality of being
human is, so a world envisaged as " motionless " does not
unveil to us its deepest reality.

But from our standpoint the history of the world falls into two parts : the past and the future, separated from each other by the elusive and ever-fleeting wall of the now. A total knowledge of the world would therefore have to encompass the past and the future; and from this it follows that a phenomenology of the world phenomenon must involve in its enquiry not only the study of the past but—in so far as such a thing is possible—the problem of the future as well.

We must try, then, to trace and capture the pattern presented by the world in a past, as well as in a future, direction.

v *Looking at Life: the Old Way and the New*

Over a long period—up to a century ago, one might almost say—exploration of the universe invariably had the appearance of a venture into space. It was a quest for the world : the size and volume of the earth, the distances between the planets, the stars and the spiral nebulae, and their positioning relative to one another. Very gradually we have come to realize that the picture thus formed in our imagination had only a fleeting moment, a mere fraction of a long succession of changing circumstances. As has so often been said, the major discovery of modern science has really been the discovery of time—of time as a constituent of everything. We differ from our ancestors not so much because we know more things than they did, but because we have discovered time and so have learnt to see everything in a new perspective.

It would take us too far afield to describe here the various notions which men down the ages have formed regarding the universe, from the days when the earth was thought to be a huge disc floating upon the waters and covered over by a vaulted "ceiling" on which the stars were fixed like so many little lanterns, kindled in the evening and snuffed out at dawn. It took mankind a very long time to reach the point where it could form a more accurate idea of the world which we inhabit; and then only by protracted study and research was our modern conception of it finally achieved.

Those old notions, however much they may have differed from one another, all had certain things in common : typical were their constricted dimensions, mechanistic structure and static character.

In the first place there were their constricted dimensions. Even in the Ptolemaic picture of things—which continued in vogue for more than a thousand years and right up to the Renaissance period was the generally accepted way of envisaging the cosmos—the earth was seen as a globe encompassed by huge crystalline spheres. It was not until our own time that men to some extent became aware of the gigantic dimensions and amazing structure of the universe.

In the next place, the old picture was dominated by a mechanistic model of the universe. By this is meant that men saw the world as a combination of heterogeneous elements that were in some way " put together " extraneously and had only an accidental link with one another. A view of this sort made no proper allowance for the reciprocal cohesion of all entities. Just as a machine is made up from a number of previously prepared components, so men imagined the world to be a huge mechanism in which a variety of pre-constituted and mutually independent entities had been conjoined artificially. The earth, the vault of heaven, the plants, animals and man were thus envisaged as so many diverse " creatures ", subsisting independently of each other, as it were, and only made up into a whole extrinsically, like, for example, the pieces of furniture in a living-room. In the modern world picture there is a complete reversal of these conditions. Science has gradually made it more and more clear that all entities are interconnected, so that we can now see the world as a mighty, organic whole in which every single thing is related to everything else. The world in which we live presents itself to us not as a machine, artificially contrived, but as an organism building itself up from within—an organism in which all entities have appeared through something like a stage by stage process of growth.

Finally, the old world picture stood for the firm belief that the universe is to be conceived of as a fundamentally changeless and static whole. Of course, men were not blind to the mutations and motions occurring in the world; but as they saw it, these changes were always on the surface of things and did not affect their essential nature. From its moment of origin everything assumed a form and aspect that were definitive and unchanging; and these forms were constant, unalterable. The machine worked, it was activated; but the machine itself never altered. Along with the mechanistic view of the world its static character has also disintegrated; so that nowadays we see the universe as an enormous historical process, an evolutive happening which has been going on for thousands of millions of years and is moving on into an incalculable future. The reason why the idea of evolution is of such great importance is that it points us to the fundamental and dynamic unity or oneness of the world.[14] Our world view, once static, has now become entirely dynamic.

So there we have the three principal characteristics of the modern view : we live in a universe gigantic in its dimensions, building itself up organically as a cohesive whole, and impelled by an inner dynamic and energy toward its completion. The old idea of things has gone beyond recall; and now the world is revealed to us in a totally new guise. For the first time we are beginning to come to terms with the revolution that this has brought about in human consciousness.

Naturally, this new picture of the world did not spring up overnight; nor has it been the outcome of one particular science. Now here, now there, the new aspects of reality have appeared. Small " pockets " of insight regarding the dynamic structure of things have been formed and then have gradually expanded until finally they have coalesced into one large whole.

Biology and its kindred sciences have contributed more even than astronomy to forming our modern conception of the world; for it is from the study of the forms of life that the idea of evolution, of a process of progressive growth, has come most clearly into prominence. This gave opportunity for the concept of evolution to spread gradually to all the other sciences and in the end to dominate and control our whole way of envisaging the world. The great pioneer in this field was Darwin; and indeed his importance goes beyond his strictly scientific theories. It was Darwin who put the idea of evolution on the map once and for all, as far as science is concerned; and since his time it has been a constant and fructifying source of insight into the world process. The publication in 1859 of *The Origin of Species* will always be one of the most significant events, therefore, in the history of Western thought.

In the wake of biology the rest of the sciences have made the concept of evolution an integral element in their outlook and approach. In physics as in the sciences of mind we have come to see that we cannot in the end understand any phenomenon whatever, unless our investigation takes into account the way in which it has come to be what it is. We now know that even the atoms have their history, the stars their birth, their prime and their decay, that languages have had their stages of development, that cultures come and cultures go. The historical dimension of everything has become evident to us with unprecedented force; so that from now on the categories of historicity are extended to cover the totality of the universe.

All this suggests that the term "evolution" can be understood in two differing senses. By "evolution" we may mean the mutations that in the course of time have taken place in the various forms of life (biological evolutionism); or we may equally well mean that the cosmos as a whole is subject to the law of evolution and that everything comes to be by a process of growth of some kind (expanded or cosmic evolution). We might say, then, that biological evolutionism has prepared the way for an expanded or cosmic evolutionism. From this standpoint biological evolutionism is only a constituent part or particular aspect of a far more comprehensive phenomenon: the evolution of the universe.

Let us now pause for a moment to consider the biological evolutionism which underlies the expanded evolutionism that Teilhard stood for. In the nineteenth century biological evolution gave rise to a great deal of discussion. Like every new idea this one had at first a lot of opposition to overcome. The reason for that cannot have been merely the built-in conservatism of so many people, but must also have something to do with the fact that the proofs advanced were in their early stages certainly open to question and that the actual thesis was quite often formulated in an inexact way. The idea of evolution had itself to undergo an evolutionary process [15] before it could present itself to us with the requisite clarity and in a proper guise. Again, the data on which it rested showed certain gaps which still had to be filled in. With the passage of time the theory of evolution has been stripped of all the philosophical speculations annexed to it and restored to the purely scientific terrain where it belongs. What is more, so many new facts have come to light, especially in the field of palaeontology, that we now command a very extensive range of material for study and are in a position to reconstruct, in its main lines, the history of life.

The present state of science no doubt leaves a great many questions still to be answered, especially with regard to the mechanism of evolution in the plant and animal kingdoms. When it comes to the factors that have contributed to the evolution of life in its various forms, we are still to a great extent groping in the dark; and the explanations proposed, however valuable they may be, cannot so far give us complete satisfaction. This makes no difference to the fact that establishing the historical " truth " of evolution is a definite achievement on the part of science and must be accepted as such. When all has been said, the position with evolution is the same as with so many other phenomena in nature : we can confidently affirm that they exist, without being able to account for their internal structure.

We have referred to biological evolution as an established " historical fact " or " truth ". This term perhaps requires

some brief clarification. In the natural sciences it is customary
to apply the word "fact" only to an occurrence or phenomenon that can be observed and controlled on an experimental
basis. On methodological grounds, therefore, some writers
prefer not to label evolution a "fact", since it is not open to
direct observation and cannot be reproduced experimentally.
They would rather speak, where evolution is concerned, of a
theory or an hypothesis. We must not be misled, however, as
to the intention of these writers—as though they had it in mind
to express the least doubt as to the reality of an evolutionary
process. It is simply and solely on a point of methodology—
and on that alone—that they wish to avoid calling evolution a
fact : that is, they want to confine the term "scientific fact"
strictly to phenomena or occurrences which can be observed and
repeated. Thus Professor L. von Bertalanffy says : "Evolution
is . . . not a fact, if by this term we mean something that is
directly observable. Rather, the idea of evolution is an extrapolation from facts, the justification for which is the vast
amount of documented evidence in its favour".[16]

In ordinary usage, however, the word "fact" has a much
wider connotation and covers events that have occurred down
the ages as well. Thus we talk of historical facts such as the
battle of Waterloo or the murder of Julius Caesar. In this
broader sense evolution is a "fact" regarding which no
scientist of repute entertains any lingering doubt.

Not all writers, however, cling to this methodological distinction. They flatly call evolution an established fact. Thus,
for instance, Professor P. P. Grassé : "To reject the idea of
evolution implies giving up any wish to understand the living
world, past and present; it means abandoning all hope of a
scientific interpretation of the order of nature, of comprehend-
ing man's origin and his place in the living world. Evolution is
not a hypothesis but a fact—such is the assured verdict, if not
of all, at any rate of the vast majority of biologists, wherever
their philosophical inclinations may lie; and it reflects the
outcome of ninety years of strenuous endeavour, ever since

the publication of *The Origin of Species,* on the part of naturalists all over the world."[17]

The eminent biologist, Professor Lucien Cuénot declares no less emphatically : " Transformism—which is as much as to say, biological evolution, is not an hypothesis, a theory or a faith--as so many incompetent polygraphs persist in assuring us. The philosophers and theologians have to acknowledge it as a firmly established fact. Biological evolution is actually just a particular instance of universal evolution ".[18]

Whilst it may be possible, therefore, to argue about what term it is appropriate to use, as to the essential, basic issue there can no longer be any serious doubt. In the view of the overwhelming majority of biologists—if not of every single one—the case for evolutionism has been settled once for all. It is surely worth noting that no one has ever been able to think of a single alternative hypothesis which would account for the evidence provided by palaeontology and comparative anatomy. No serious person could think of going back to Cuvier's theory of successive creations.

In constructing his world view, therefore, Teilhard had every right to make his appeal to the historical fact of evolution. Any other possibility simply does not exist; and this is in fact true not only for biological evolutionism but for " expanded evolution " as well. Anybody attempting to raise objections to the fact would merely reveal how out of touch he was with the present state of scientific knowledge. There too the scientific substructure is so solid and unassailable that any criticism of him on this score would seem to us to be ruled out.

Teilhard was consequently justified in saying that the world presents itself to us not only as a system in motion (which we find also with the machine) but as a system in process of becoming and of growth—which is quite a different thing.[19]

We have to learn to see man also within this universal process of becoming, in order to discover the place that he occupies in the cosmos and to estimate at their true importance both the fact of his intimate connection with the world around him and his character as a unique and exceptional being; for even man has countless threads binding him fast to the world around, however much he may transcend his environment. To employ an image of Julian Huxley's : the earth is not simply a pedestal on which man is set like a statue, but rather a gigantic stalk on which man is the flower.

Man and world, then, cannot be viewed in isolation from each other. Man forms a constituent part, an aspect of the world, and is the highest expression of the energies operative in that world. It is indeed remarkable that even in the sciences this cohesion of man and world was lost sight of for so long. Men built a science of the cosmos without reckoning with man; and they studied man without linking him with the world. But a science of the world and of men—envisaged as a unity—nobody had ever ventured upon.[20] An authentic phenomenology of the cosmic must therefore include man within the scope of its reflection, must even in large measure concentrate its attention upon him. To set out to comprehend the world without bringing man into the picture must result in a thoroughly mutilated notion of the world and make it impossible for us to see the world in its totality.

As Teilhard conceived it, " the phenomenon of man " is of capital and central importance for arriving at a right concept of the world. The whole of evolution has moved *de facto* in the direction of man, has led up to the emergence of man, who forms the crown and climax of it. So it is from this standpoint alone that the world can be understood in its innermost being —in so far, that is, as we confine ourselves to the phenomenological scheme. The phenomenon " world " will not be fully intelligible to the objective observer, unless he involves the phenomenon " man " in his analysis—nay, more, unless he concedes to this phenomenon of man the first, salient, key position.

The point of departure, then, for Teilhard's world view is clear enough : the universe presents itself to the eye of the beholder as a four-dimensional continuum, extended in space and time, an organically cohesive and evolving whole which is most completely self-manifested in man and so is best to be understood in that context and perspective.

Chapter 2

"AN IMMENSE PSYCHIC EXERCISE"

To obtain our notion of the universe we have to confine ourselves virtually to a study of this earth. We can in fact take
this planet as a typical sample of what the universe is like.
About the phenomena belonging to other planets and about
what may have happened there down the aeons of time we as
yet know very little indeed. In the present state of our knowledge it would seem permissible to generalize—up to a point—
certain overall features of our earth and extend them, analogically, to other planets. But we would prefer to leave that question aside here and stick to what we can recognize as actual
fact.

i *The Three Phases or Spheres*

The history of our planet appears to us as a continuous and
uninterrupted flow of events and changing conditions. From
the unity and coherence of this evolutive process it follows
that every classification we make in terms of epochs and stages
is bound to be more or less artificial. Yet it is justified in that
it enables the spectator to see important occurrences in a proper
light and to understand better the nature of the course taken
by the earth's history. If we glance at the history of our earth
it soon becomes apparent that there have been three very different and clearly distinguishable elements or stages in it.
What appears to us as a first phase is the period during which
the earth's crust solidified after a process of cooling down. No
trace of life is as yet detectable; nor—because of the tremendous heat—was it yet possible. Some believe that our earth

and the other planets of our galaxy must have originated from the extinction and breaking up of a " twin sun ". The distinctive thing about this first phase, then, was the exclusive presence of inorganic matter.

The second period begins when life first emerges and the various forms of life gradually unfold. So far we have not been able to say for certain just when the first manifestations of life occurred on earth. As a minimal limit we have to reckon with about two thousand million years; and some experts think that the first organic matter originated as much as three thousand million years ago or perhaps even earlier still. Fossils which are clearly observable evidence can take us back about 700 million years; but geochemistry permits us to go much further than that. The schizophytes (bacteria, blue algae) are commonly referred to as being the oldest forms of life, so that the pre-Cambrian age has sometimes been called the schizophytic era. The bifurcation of the plant and animal kingdoms happened early on; and by the Cambrian age we find most of the phyla already constituted. The animal kingdom in its turn bifurcated at a very early stage into the vertebrate and invertebrate animals. During Palaeozoic times the trilobites and fishes predominated in the animal world; and then in the Mesozoic period the ascendancy passed to the reptiles who, in the bisexual variety, took over the dry land. At the close of this epoch there appeared first the birds and then the mammals, whose major advances and development were to occur during the Neozoic period. Palaeontology has afforded an abundance of data to illustrate this whole course of events.

The second phase, then, is characterized by the emergence and marvellous upsurge and progress of life, which added an entirely new aspect to our earth, encircling it with a wonderful covering of plant growth and populating it with an infinite variety of changing forms of life : the biosphere, a band of life enveloping the world. But about five or six hundred thousand years ago a new phenomenon made its entry—a phenomenon so novel and so potent that before very long it had begun to change the face of the earth and to add a further

dimension to it : the dimension of mind. From his source in
the biosphere man entered upon the terrestrial scene; and this
event soon came to have such central and all-embracing significance that it can only be described as a new stage in the
world's history. Our earth acquired a second "envelope" :
the envelope of mind, the noosphere.

The researches of the palaeontologists have already brought
to light some very material data regarding the process by which
man came to be what he now is—although a great many problems obviously still remain unsolved.[21] That man, looked at
biologically, was a product of the higher animal kingdom is
for the vast majority of experts in this field a fact no longer
open to question. Hardly a year passes without new discoveries
being made which reinforce this view and serve to fill in our
picture of the evolutionary process. As we said earlier on,
Teilhard had himself a very important part in this research
into the origins of man.

All this would seem to point to the justice of dividing the
world's history into three phases. The emergence of life and
the advent of man were really capital events which in each
case signify an enormous jump in evolution, and in comparison
with which all the other changes that have taken place—
whether of a geological, biological or even anthropological
character—can only be considered as of secondary importance.
The three major steps in the " eventualizing " of the world are
summed up, therefore, in the three words : matter, life, mind.
They also serve to indicate the three spheres which we encounter around us and which evidently express the totality of
our cosmos.

ii *The Crucial Moments in this Evolution*

Every change, every mutation—whether geological, biological
or cultural—which the passage of time has brought in its train
presents science with a complex problem. Not only must it try
to establish what such changes were, but it must also attempt

to trace their causes and to find out what they imply for the course of events as a whole. Among the many changes that have taken place on earth through the ages there are two especially which command our attention and are indeed of fundamental importance : the first of these events is the emergence of life, the second the breaking through of mind, the coming to birth of man. These events constitute the two "hinges" of history, of cosmic history as we now envisage it. They form the points of junction between the three phases or spheres which we were considering a moment ago.

There is a fundamental distinction to be drawn between matter and life, between animal life and man; but notwithstanding that, there is also a radical bond and an intrinsic cohesion between these three spheres. This must be immediately obvious to us when we reflect that vegetal and animal life is contingent upon all sorts of chemical elements and that man's existence too links him with the world around him. Our bodies are made up of atoms and molecules; and we are in continual need of nourishment, which we get from the plant and animal kingdoms.

Much more problematical and complex, however, is the question as to whether it is possible to speak of a genetic link between these three spheres—of the biosphere as having originated from the geosphere, and the noosphere from the biosphere. This question is all the more difficult to answer in that it raises not only scientific but philosophical and theological issues as well—particularly where man is concerned. Still, we should not lose sight of the fact that Teilhard is determined to stick to the terrain of science here and deliberately leaves the philosophical and theological implications to those more competent to handle them.[22] His aim is in fact to devise a phenomenology of the cosmic, and not to construct a metaphysics or a theology. Let us look at the connection between the three spheres, therefore, simply and solely as that presents itself to observation.

The prevailing scientific view is that a gradual transition from the geosphere to the biosphere—or, to put it another way,

from inorganic to organic matter—is to be regarded if not as a
complete certainty, at any rate as being highly probable. Of
course, it cannot at this moment be scientifically proved that
life must have arisen from matter by a gradual chemical process, any more than it can be scientifically demonstrated that
such a transition must have been impossible. The position
now reached in this particular field of enquiry may perhaps
best be summarized as follows : that a transition took place
from inorganic matter to organic matter and life cannot as yet
be completely proved; but it is accepted as a working hypothesis by all scientific investigators. A transition of that sort is
in their opinion the most reasonable and most likely explanation for the origin of life. It is along such lines, therefore,
that research continues; and some very material evidence has
already been brought to light.[23] It is not unreasonable to hope
and expect that sooner or later we shall reach a solution to
this problem.

   That being so, did Teilhard lay himself open to censure for
having postulated in his world view such a transition from
inanimate to animate matter, from megamolecule to micro-
organism? We think not. Without this hypothesis a phenomenological account of the universe would seem to be impossible. If one looks at the history of the world in a purely
phenomenological plane, abstracting any philosophical or
theological standpoint, then the emergence of the earliest life
presents the appearance of an event in the womb of matter;
and any account of it will be in terms of natural causation. So
in *The Phenomenon of Man* Teilhard set out, if not to prove
or explain the transition from inorganic to organic matter, at
least to show how plausible it is. As he saw it, the beginnings
of life are to be seen as the product or outcome of a kind of
maturation process in matter : " In every domain, when anything exceeds a certain measurement, it suddenly changes its
aspect, condition or nature. The curve doubles back, the surface contracts to a point, the solid disintegrates, the liquid
boils, the germ cell divides, intuition suddenly bursts on the
piled up facts . . . Critical points have been reached, rungs on

the ladder, involving a change of state—jumps of all sorts *in the course* of development. Henceforward this is the *only* way in which science can speak of a " first instant ". But it is none the less a *true way* ".[24]

Thus the emergence of life is to be seen as a critical moment, a phase-mutation in the history of the earth, comparable (in a backward direction) only with the coming into existence of the atoms themselves from the sub- or pre-atomic elements : " Protoplasm was formed once and once only on earth, just as nuclei and electrons were formed once and once only in the cosmos."[25]

Much later, when life had gradually developed and had reached a high degree of complexity, an equally critical phase-mutation was to occur once more in the mighty process of evolution : after matter had been vitalized, life was now to be "hominized". An utterly new phenomenon was manifested in the womb of life : the entry of man.

We are faced here with a new and extremely complex and many-faceted problem. Despite his original and irreducible attributes man cannot be envisaged as a completely heterogeneous being that made its appearance in the world *ab extra*, as it were, and entirely unrelated to the entities all around it. On the contrary, we find that when man does appear, it is in intimate association with the animal kingdom. Quite logically, therefore, a phenomenological study of man's first arrival on the scene will stress the links connecting him with the rest of the cosmos; but in so doing it will of course not lose sight of the quality of originality in man. What differentiates man from the world around him and is his exclusive privilege is his power of conscious reflection; but that does not preclude his being linked in innumerable ways with the higher animal kingdom.[26] Comparative anatomy has made us aware that our organism is constructed on the same basic design as that of the higher animals and that the human body still bears traces of the evolution undergone by the chordates. Palaeontology too has been able to disclose a number of important links, from the course of human evolution; and new evidence calculated to shed further light on our origins is continually turning up. These facts, among others, make it really impossible to doubt any longer the connection between the other animate creatures and ourselves. Again, therefore, we are confronted at this point with a highly crucial moment in the earth's history, a moment of capital significance, when the cosmos assumed a new dimension: the dimension of mind.

Teilhard is clear and emphatic in making the distinction between man and animal: "We are separated by a chasm— or a threshold—which it cannot cross. Because we are reflective we are not only different but quite other. It is not a matter of change of degree, but of a change of nature, resulting from a change of state."[27] With man life does indeed enter upon a new phase, the phase of reflective, conscious being. But that is not the end of the matter. If we are going to abide by the phenomenological method as described earlier on, then without prejudice to a possible further explanation we must try to understand this phenomenon of reflective consciousness within the totality of cosmic evolution. Life arose in the womb of matter; and this life has "fanned out" into ever more and more complex forms. It is not just the forms of outward manifestation that are involved here. Even more important is the diversity (in the animal kingdom, at any rate) evident in psychism. To interpret this psychism as a uniform and undifferentiated phenomenon would be a great mistake. Instinct is to be thought of as a variable dimension: ". . . there is not *one* instinct in nature, but a multitude of forms of instincts each corresponding to a particular solution of the problem of life. The 'psychical' make-up of an insect is not and cannot be that of a vertebrate; nor can the instinct of a squirrel be that of a cat or an elephant: this in virtue of the position of each on the tree of life . . . The mind (or psyche) of a dog, despite all that may be said to the contrary, is positively superior to that of a mole or fish."[28]

Once we recognize this diversity, this *gradation*, in animal psychism, it becomes clear that viewed in its psychic aspect the animal kingdom forms in itself an ascending system, " a kind of fan-like structure in which the higher terms on each nervure are recognized each time by a greater range of choice and depending on a better defined centre of co-ordination and consciousness ".[29] Between this consciousness of the most highly developed animal and the reflective consciousness of man there occurred (whether for extrinsic or intrinsic reasons we do not propose to consider here) a critical phase-shift whereby life attained to a higher stage and assumed a new aspect.

Just as in the case of the emergence of the earliest life, so too regarding the first beginnings of man, therefore, we are entitled to speak of *a discontinuity in the continuity*. The current of life flows onward without interruption; and on the face of it little is changed. Reproduction, multiplication, ramification, nutrition, death—with man all these processes go on as they had with the animals before him. Yet deep down a change has taken place : the life-stream is not what it had formerly been, it is not the same, now that it has crossed the barrier of reflection : from now on it is to prove the source of wholly new created entities, previously quite inconceivable :[30] " The being who is the object of his own reflection, in consequence of that very doubling back upon himself, becomes in a flash able to raise himself into a new sphere. In reality, another world is born. Abstraction, logic, reasoned choice and inventions, mathematics, art, calculation of space and time, anxieties and dreams of love—all these activities of *inner life* are nothing else than the effervescence of the newly-formed centre as it explodes onto itself."[31]

Psychism has been ever more clearly manifested throughout the animal world. Just where it begins we cannot possibly say. The further down we go in the direction of the more primitive forms, the vaguer it becomes—and the more difficult to detect. If, however, we take the opposite direction—the path which history has also taken—then we find it pursuing an onward course, ever more apparent and many-sided until in the highest animals it attains almost to the *frontiers of intelligence*. When this psychic concentration had reached its greatest intensity, there ensued the critical moment, the phase-mutation, out of which man emerges.

How this process was realized concretely we shall doubtless never know—just as we shall never be able to comprehend how intelligence is awakened in any child.[32]

iii *The Law of Increasing Complexity and Increasing Consciousness*

The universe presents itself to us as a history, a succession of events, in which we have found the most important moments to be: the build-up of matter, the vitalization of matter and the hominization of life. With these three moments correspond the three phases or spheres which we have described. Of course, up to a point such a classification is artificial, since everything constitutes a continuous whole and invites us to see it as a continuity.

When we contemplate the process of evolution that has occurred on our planet, we naturally find ourselves asking whether that process, taken as a whole, shows any kind of intrinsic orientation. Teilhard thinks that it does. The course of evolution does not look to be a disorderly succession of events, a see-saw movement or a swinging to and fro between different poles, but rather a gradual ascent, set irreversibly in one direction. Let this not be misunderstood, however. The question at issue here is not whether the evolutionary process is being guided from outside in a particular direction by a Higher Being toward a predetermined goal. A philosophical finalism of that sort lies outside the compass of the natural sciences and therefore is not something that we should consider here at all. The question posed here relates only to the sequence which has, as a matter of fact, been manifested in the phenomena. *De facto*, we see evolution taking a particular path which issues eventually in man.

If we contemplate the whole sweep of evolution, it must strike us at once that the course taken by the world as a whole has all the time been moving in the direction of what is more complex. It invariably proceeds from simpler to more intricate structures—from elementary particles to atom, from atom to molecule, from molecule to cell, from the cell to the pluricellular creatures, from the most primitive of these to more and more complex organisms, ending up with the most complex entity that we have in our world : man—the being in whom all prior forms of complexity are repeated and surpassed. A third infinity would seem to be manifested here; besides the infinite progression to larger and to smaller, one that tends to what is complex.

It looks as though the whole course of the world's history is orientated toward the building up of conditions of ever greater complexity. By this increasing complexity we mean not so much the fact that as one thing or one creature succeeds another in the passage of time they are equipped with more and more intricate mechanisms, but rather that they exhibit a greater richness of internal organization and manifest in their structure an ever greater degree of intrinsic unity and quality of concentration. Now this increasing complexity is not a philosophical theory or an *a priori* principle or a vague speculation, but something quite factual and objective established by the natural scientist. It is an incontrovertible fact that the whole evolutionary process, the traces of which are everywhere around us, has moved in this direction—in the direction, that is, of an increasing complexity.

To substantiate this we cannot do better than remind ourselves of the following chronological series of phenomena : the spiral nebulae from which the universe is built up consist principally of hydrogen atoms (preceded by the elementary particles : protons, neutrons, electrons, photons, etc.). In the spiral nebulae condensations occur which we call stars and in which the hydrogen atoms are converted into helium and a number of other more complex elements. From the defunct stars the planets then originate. Now it is precisely in the

planets—and principally on their outermost crust—that we
encounter the largest number of elements, and the most complex ones too, giving rise to an unlimited diversity of chemical
combinations. On the surface of the planets—and only there
—appear the primary forms of life, which in turn become
continually more complex; until finally in the most complex
beings of all—namely, in men—self-consciousness and freedom emerge. Anyone who considers these phenomena in the
order we have indicated can scarcely avoid the impression that
a part of the stuff of the universe, by virtue of an inner dynamic
(called by Teilhard " radial energy ") collects and concentrates
itself, as it were, to an ever greater degree of intensity. " Historically, the stuff of the universe goes on becoming concentrated into ever more organized forms of matter."[33] We may
regard this phenomenon, then, as a process of " involution "
(*enroulement*) and interiorization. In this way organized entities emerge, held together by their own energy and each of
them forming a self-contained, equilibrial system. One thinks
here of atoms, molecules, cells, pluricellular creatures, human
individuals. All these constitute so many examples of self-
contained systems in a state of equilibrium, which are the
product of a general process of involution.

But having established that, we have still taken into account
only one aspect of reality; for running parallel to the increasing complexification there is a second distinguishing feature of
evolution : namely, an orientation toward an ever increasing
degree of consciousness. Throughout the whole long, evolutive
process there is a gradual growth of psychic manifestation,
supported by the steady advance to perfection of the nervous
system and reaching its point of climax in man. If we survey
the course of animal evolution as a whole, it is surely evident
that this entire process is marked by a gradual refining and
extension of the nervous system, and especially of the brain
system. The phenomenon of cerebralization, the proportional
development of the brain vis-à-vis the whole organism, gives
us a key which helps to explain or clarify the direction taken

by biological evolution generally. Thus running through the forms in which it has been manifested—however many and various they may be—we can discern, alongside an increasing complexity, an increase, a gradual growth, of psychism; and this helps us a great deal in forming a correct idea of evolution itself.

So we have two phenomena here : increasing complexity and expanding or ascending psychism. Both are susceptible of direct and objective observation on the part of the natural scientist. But immediately the question arises as to whether there is some intrinsic connection between the two phenomena —as though we are to think of the second as being of necessity dependent or conditional upon the first. We need to be careful how we answer this question. First of all, we should note the word of warning sounded by F. M. Bergounioux[34] in these terms : " Appealing to the ' complexification-consciousness' phenomenon means that we resort to a philosophical explanation. Even if we postulate a link between the two states—between the complexity of morphological groupings and an increase of consciousness—sound logic still does not permit us to say that the relation between them is one of causality." No one, surely, will deny that it is wrong to infer causal connection from a parallelism—that would be to commit the common fallacy : *cum hoc, ergo propter hoc.* On a strictly scientific basis all we can do is to take note of the fact that the two phenomena occur simultaneously. The fact that an increasing complexity—especially of the nervous system— and an expanding psychism and consciousness always occur together is in itself no proof that the one is a consequence of the other. The most one could say is that, granted the constant parallelism between the two, such a relationship is strongly to be suspected.

If it is the case, then, that we cannot simply affirm a connection between complexity and psychism, it cannot be denied, either, that exploring the precise relationship between them must be treated as a purely scientific project and that philo-

sophical argument, of whatever kind, must be left aside. We
may yet learn a good deal about the nature of this relationship
from neurophysiology. Man—as philosophers nowadays
would say—is an incarnated consciousness. In him mind and
matter constitute a substantial unity. Even the most sublime
expressions of the human mind have an organic aspect, a
physiological infrastructure. Even though "the life of the
mind" cannot be reduced to that infrastructure, it would be
wrong to pretend that the latter is of no consequence to our
mental activity.

When, therefore, Teilhard stresses the connection between
organic complexity and psychism, he is entirely in line with
modern science. For that reason we believe that Père Bergounioux's argument is really based on a misunderstanding.
Obviously, Teilhard has no intention of asserting that psychism
is dependent simply and solely on the degree of organic complexity—as though forcing a machine's complexity up to a high
enough pitch would suffice automatically to give it a consciousness of the same character as man's. He never countenanced
any such idea. If he had any preconception regarding a connection between organic complexity and consciousness it must
be understood in this sense : that each and every degree of
consciousness always presupposes an equivalent degree of
organic complexity, of interior unity and concentration. Without such organic complexity psychic life is not possible; and
the higher the form of psychic life, the greater the integrated
unity and complexity of the organism has to be. Thus the
integration-mechanisms of the unified being discharge an indispensable role here. All this is completely in line with
modern neurophysiology, which has quite clearly demonstrated
that the degree of psychism and consciousness is always conditioned by the degree to which a given organism has an
integrated unity.[35]

Once we have established in this way that in every living
creature there is a demonstrable link between organic complexity and psychism, the next obvious step is to try and

examine this phenomenon in its historical dimension too. As a palaeontologist, Teilhard was an obvious person to set this aspect of living entities in a sharp light; for the palaeontologist sees in the history of life a persisting increase of complexity and psychism. As modern biology has demonstrated the indispensable connection of both phenomena, he was fully justified in projecting this into the historical process of evolution as well, without thereby in any way overstepping the boundaries of science. The law formulated by him is a purely scientific one, therefore; and there is nothing philosophical about it.[36] It goes without saying, of course, that the word " consciousness " in the foregoing passage is to be understood in its broadest sense, as indicating " every kind of psychism, from the most rudimentary forms of interior perception imaginable to the human phenomenon of reflective thought ".[37]

On purely phenomenological grounds, then, " we may be sure that every time a richer and better organized structure will correspond to the more developed consciousness ".[38] The fact that consciousness and complexity of organization go hand in hand is taken by Teilhard as a " parameter ", a yardstick, which allows us to follow the course of evolution and " to connect both the internal and the external films of the world, not only *in their position* (point by point), but also ... in their motion ".[39] Thence also his conclusion : " *Spiritual perfection (or conscious ' centreity ') and material synthesis (or complexity) are but the two aspects or connected parts of one and the same phenomenon.*"[40]

This conclusion is highly material to Teilhard's picture of the world. It brings us, in fact, to the very centre of his system. The law of complexity-consciousness is important not merely because, as we shall see later on, it permits us to look into the future to some extent, but above all because it sheds such a clear light on the major place assigned by Teilhard to the " within " of things, and to psychism in the structure of the world. The world stuff—he never ceases to tell us—exhibits

two aspects and is to be envisaged as two-sided. The
interiority, the within of things, psychism, consciousness (in
its widest sense)—this too is a cosmic phenomenon which
has to be included in a phenomenology of the universe and
assigned its due place within the whole. Until now such
a thing has hardly been attempted, because the phenomenon
of consciousness has always been thought of as being confined to the highest forms of life and has almost invariably
been treated as a marginal phenomenon of limited significance.[41] "Consciousness, in order to be integrated into a
world system, necessitates consideration of the existence of a
new aspect or dimension in the stuff of the universe."[42]

In everything, therefore, Teilhard distinguishes a double
aspect : an exterior, which relates only to the observable connections and dimensions of material things, and an interior—
an interior aspect of things, which is to be envisaged as co-
extensive with their exterior and in some degree is present in
them all. This "inside", this interiority, we perceive clearly
enough in ourselves—it is a privilege *par excellence* of man—
but in a different yet equally real fashion it is undeniably
present in the higher animals as well. However, the further we
descend in the animal and plant kingdoms toward the more
primitive forms of life—right down to the unicellular creatures—the more difficult this interiority is to observe, even
though its existence there cannot be disproved. Even a living
cell reacts differently to its environment from a molecule.
Eventually, this interiority of things gets lost in the mysterious
depths of matter.

Thus there are degrees of consciousness, degrees of the
organic integration of things; and to the extent that this inner
complexity increases we find higher and higher—and totally
new—qualities being manifested. That is not to say—as has
been said from time to time—that Teilhard is an advocate of
pan-psychism—as though one and the same consciousness were
present in all things : in the atom, the amoeba, plant, animal,
man. That would be a total misrepresentation of what he has

in mind. What he means is simply this : that if we want to arrive at a coherent account of the universe—one based on a scientific phenomenology—we must accept that, albeit in an analogous fashion and in varying degree, all creatures possess a certain interiority, an interior aspect.

All this goes to show what an important place the law of increasing complexity and expanding consciousness has in Teilhard's system. It is this law that in his view affords us the key to a correct idea of evolution—which in its turn is a central phenomenon, apart from which the universe cannot be integrated.

iv *The Place of Man in the Universe*

To anyone who contemplates the world simply as a phenomenon, the universe appears as a coherent whole which has evolved in a particular direction. The universe, seen as a historical process, presents itself to us as an ascent toward ever higher states of consciousness. As we have seen already, evolution manifestly tends in a particular direction : *de facto*, it has moved in the direction of mind.

Once we have seen and understood this, we can have a better idea of man's position within the evolving universe.

There was a time when man was envisaged as being completely separate and detached from his natural environment. He was a spectator; and nature was the object of his contemplation. The earth was of course regarded as the centre of the cosmos; and man's place on it was that of lord and master, to whom everything else was subject. All things were made for him; and he could exploit them to his own advantage. He was like a feudal overlord; and the world, he felt, was his in fee.

After the activities of Galileo—and even more of Darwin —that idea had to go. Man lost not only his central place in the universe but also his independent status vis-à-vis his natural environment. Among the earliest Darwinians and

their immediate followers man was usually regarded as an
accidental " offshoot " of the animal kingdom, a member of
the group of primates; and any difference between him and
them was a matter of degree only. Man here was completely
engulfed in nature; and of his character as an original being
nothing remained at all.

But that idea too has had its day. Biologists nowadays are
beginning to form a new conception of man's relationship to
his natural environment.[43] No longer is he to be regarded as
an insignificant by-product of the animal kingdom, however
close his links with it may be. Anatomically, no doubt, he has
a considerable affinity with the higher animals. Historically
speaking, he is the latest arrival in the realm of living creatures; and his roots are buried in the remote history of the
animal kingdom. Yet he makes his appearance in the world
as a phenomenon, irreducible and altogether new, which adds
to that world another aspect—the aspect of reflective consciousness and of freedom—and before long changes the whole
prospect presented by the earth. With man—as we said
before—there dawns a new phase of the world's history : it is
encompassed by a new " sphere ". In man and in him alone
(so far as we know) the world becomes conscious of itself.

That man does, after all, occupy an exceptional position in
the cosmos has once again become apparent, therefore. The
truth is that his place is a central one—in a context not of
stability but of movement, since evolution means an ascent
to consciousness and freedom, supported by an ever greater
complexity of the nervous system and the brain. Because of
this man really does stand at the head of nature, of that
environment which he dominates, investigates and uses as he
will. Henceforward he is to be the pivot of evolution, occupy-
ing as he does the furthest outpost within it.

Indeed, in the perspective of such a dynamic view of the
world it is no longer possible to see man as a marginal phenomenon in the whole range of things and events or as the
accidental product of blind natural forces. His position in the
evolutive process going on in the world—a process regulated

from within by principles now known to us—is too central for that. Thus modern science, which at first deprived man of his central position, has now restored it to him—but on a far more exalted basis. Man is as it were the spearhead of evolution; and from a phenomenological standpoint it is this that gives him his status of dignity and superiority over his natural surroundings.

The thought that there may be yet other planets in the universe on which life has evolved in no way detracts from this idea. Even on the supposition that there may be creatures on those planets who enjoy a reflective consciousness and free will, it still remains true that the axis of world evolution passes through the beings possessed of such a consciousness. So far from constituting a difficulty for Teilhard's theory, the existence of living and intelligent beings on other planets would serve admirably to corroborate and confirm his ideas. It would surely make it evident that wherever the possibility has occurred, evolution has moved in the same direction that we have noted here on earth: in the direction, that is, of increasing " complexification " and growing consciousness. Whether there is life on other planets, however, cannot for the present be either established or denied. We can only say that it would appear to be not unlikely.

Evidently, then, in the light of our reflections so far, man is to be seen as the farthest point attained by the evolutionary process on this earth of ours. He is the crown and the (provisional) end of a long course of events. Over many millions of years nature has been at work shaping and fashioning him. But this course of events is not at an end. We have no reason to think that cosmogenesis has now reached its full and final term and that from now on everything will stay just as it is until the end of time. Evolution moves on; and so far as we can see, it stretches out into the unfathomable future. Why should the laws that have governed the past all of a sudden lose their force and cease to have any validity for the times to come?

But if world history is continuing in the direction in which it has all the time been moving, then it is with man that responsibility for the future rests; it is in and through man that the world moves on toward greater completion. In the world as we know it man is the only being wholly orientated to the future. In matter we observe a gradual process of degradation (entropy) and disintegration. In the plant and animal kingdoms an apparent stagnation has set in : many species have died out already or are on the verge of doing so. Nowhere do we see any signs of new species coming on to the scene.

Man, on the other hand, moves steadily onward and upward. As a species he shows no trace of any loss of vital energy. Numerically, he is still on the increase. His mental activity and his urge to expand are always intensifying. Of all sources of energy in the world he is the most dynamic, subjugating every other force and putting it to the service of his own efforts to make progress. Such dynamic behaviour on the part of the human species fits splendidly into the general picture that we have formed of the world. Through man as the highest and central phenomenon that world evolution has produced that same evolution is bound to follow its ascending course. It could hardly be otherwise. As a conscious and free being, man stands now at the apex of cosmogenesis. He is a " terminus " —but also a new beginning. By exerting his creative energies he will surely do his part toward completing the evolutionary process. Within the framework of the fundamental laws of nature man is the architect of to-morrow's world.

Chapter 3

THE FUTURE LOOK OF THE UNIVERSE

In the preceding chapter we set out to sketch in broad outline what the universe looks like to the observer who has obtained his picture of it from a study of past events. Fundamentally, essentially, the world appears as a historical process, as an ascent from matter to life, from life to mind. From this course of development we are able to conclude that it is possible to distinguish a dual aspect in everything : a " without " (exteriority), imbued with a centrifugal drive causing it to unfold or to " fan out " in all directions, and a " within " (interiority), characterized by a centripetal drive tending to a psychic concentration. On this canvas the various forms of life have evolved and man has eventually made his appearance as the being that unites in itself the greatest complexity and the highest type of consciousness. The whole of evolution, therefore, exhibits a line of ascent in the direction of ever greater complexity and higher consciousness : its inner orientation is centred on mind.

All this we can learn from a study of the past. But so far we have been looking at only a part of cosmic evolution—the part which belongs irrevocably to the past and can no longer be altered in any respect. If, however, we want to understand the world in its totality, we must take a look at the other side of the picture and give our attention to the future. The fact is that evolution is not marking time : the evolutive process in which we are involved and now occupy a central position moves on toward its ultimate completion. The principle of evolution once accepted, we cannot avoid being confronted with the question of the future. We are obliged by the inner dynamic of evolutionism to face up to this question.

It is a problem which Teilhard could hardly have failed to encounter; and it turns up in his very first essays, dating from as early as 1916. It looms ever larger in his thinking as the years pass; and in the latest period of his life it is right in the forefront. There can be no doubt, therefore, that he valued this part of his work especially—and regarded it indeed as perhaps the most original part of the whole. His vision of the future was for him the major discovery of his life; so that if we were to excise from his work these views that he held concerning the future—or were to thrust them aside as of minor importance—his whole picture of the world would be very considerably mutilated and robbed of one of its essential elements.

Even so, his ideas about the future are the very thing that has prompted the most criticism. A good many people who have been able to follow him and concur with his ideas thus far feel themselves beset with a degree of hesitation the moment they come up against this new stage in his thinking. Because they are anxious not to overstep the bounds of science and want to close the door to all speculations of a subjective kind, they cannot help wondering whether it is not better for the scientist to limit himself to studying the past and the present. Is it not entirely out of the question to make any scientific assessment where the future is concerned; and is not this whole area rather one for the exercise of fantasy and imagination? What are we to make, then, of this kind of speculation regarding the future?

In view of all this it may be useful if before taking a closer look at this new problem we start by examining the motives which led Teilhard to express the views which he did express about the future and also the methodological principles which such activity presupposes. This will surely help us to get a better understanding and to reach a fairer judgment of the way his mind worked in this respect.

i *The Future as an Object of Science*

What were the motives that led Teilhard to pose the problem
of man's future with such emphasis; and on what grounds did
he hold such an undertaking to be justified?

Let it be said first of all that his motives and grounds are
markedly different from those which prompt so many authors
nowadays to tell us what they think about the future of mankind. The question of what the direction or orientation of
history may be has been under discussion ever since the time
of Hegel and Marx; and over the years we have been treated
to various dissertations on this subject, some of them much to
the point, but others again very superficial and irresponsible.
Despite all the disillusion, and notwithstanding all the mistakes which have been made, people have been giving more
and more thought to this question of the future—not only
in order to find some appropriate line of conduct and some
incentive to action, but also because man today has become
aware of his historicity and in particular of his responsibility
toward the men of tomorrow. He has reached a point in his
history when he must take his destiny into his own hands and
can no longer leave it to the blind play of natural forces to
underwrite his continued existence. So this awareness on
our part of our responsibility for the future is one of the
characteristic things about our time. In very recent years it
has caught the attention and interest of innumerable thinkers
and scholars and men of science. Nobel prizewinners like Sir
George Thomson, historians like Arnold Toynbee, philosophers like Karl Jaspers and Calvo-Serer, economists like
Jean Fourastié, and many others prominent in cultural and
intellectual life to-day have written at length about their expectations regarding the future. The theme of man's historicity has become one of the central issues in contemporary
philosophy. Not without reason does Gerhard Kruger begin
his essay on "*Die Geschichte im Denken der Gegenwart*"

with the words : " History is now our greatest problem ". We
cannot fail to notice that at no time in history has man reflected to deeply about the future as he does today.

Teilhard's work in this field is wholly in line, therefore,
with the intellectual preoccupations of our century; and yet it
differs fundamentally from each of the enterprises above-
mentioned; for they were all undertaken with a particular
area and an immediate future in view. Demographers, for
instance, using statistical data as a basis, calculate what is
likely to be the increase in the human race during the next few
centuries. Historians of culture examine the chances of survival
of particular institutions or forms of culture. The question is
mooted as to the future development of science or art or
technics or social conditions generally. People are especially concerned about the prospects for Western civilization;
and they weigh the pros and cons of its survival. Obviously,
in all these instances the problem under consideration is only
a limited one; and what is being dealt with is only a small
fraction of what might be called the further development of
mankind as a biological group—quite apart from the fact that
a lot of these ruminations have a purely subjective basis.

Teilhard adopts an entirely different standpoint. He is not
concerned to know how this or that aspect of man's life may
change or be modified in the next century or so, or even to
know how art and science, European civilization and living
standards generally may evolve. The object of his attention
is not man as an individual or as representing a particular
form of culture. His standpoint is not the philosopher's, the
historian's or the economist's, but that of the geologist and
palaeontologist—that is to say, of the scientist who because of
his training and study is the most obvious person to cover the
whole range of the cosmic process. If the historian, the philosopher and the sociologist have a right to ponder the future,
why should the same right be denied to the palaeontologist,
who more than anyone else has a panoramic view of the past
and is the most conversant with the more fundamental laws
governing the whole of cosmic evolution?

When Teilhard talks to us about the future of man, what he has in mind is the future of the human race as a biological group—a group whose origins and remote history and gradual development he had studied with the greatest possible care : "Like every living creature, man has sprung into being not merely as an individual but also as a species. This is our justification for recognizing and studying in him not just the cycle of the individual but the cycle of the species too."[44] Any ideas which he had regarding the future are therefore to be understood and assessed in terms of the species. As biologist, historian, nay more, as a phenomenologist of the cosmic, he asks how the human species, in which evolution has reached its highest point, is going to develop from now on. That the historical process in which we are implicated moves forward on its evolutive course is simply a fact. Are we not automatically confronted, then, with the question : in which direction is this process of evolution going to move?

The first ground of his concern with the problem of the future of the human species is implicit in the inner dynamic of his view of the world as an evolutionary process. A second reason, however, has to do with our conduct. Up to now evolution has been accomplished passively, so to speak. Not only matter but the plants and animals—and even man himself—have evolved without actually being conscious of the process—thrust forward by an intrinsic drive, by a mysterious energy pent up in creation from the outset. That interior energy—manifested in two aspects, as centrifugal and as centripetal force—gave rise to the increasing upward movement of consciousness and also to the enormous diversity of its forms, without relying on conscious creation for voluntary effort. We have undergone evolution much more than we have helped in the process of bringing it about. But is it not beginning to look as though a fundamental change has now entered into the situation? Both because of what we now know about the past on the one hand and because of our technical potential on the other a radical transformation has come about in the human condition. Man has at last come to be aware of his

task in history and of the powers latent within him. Do we
not sense that a new sort of life has begun already and know
that as we contemplate its first awakening we are filled with
anxiety and astonishment; that something seems to be changing in the very structure of life itself? Never in all the long
centuries since it came into being has mankind generated so
much activity of mind and intellect—especially in the field of
science—as in our own day. Is all this activity, then, to no
purpose? Does it signify nothing? And is it no essential
part or consequence of this activity that we should know what
its aim is and what orientation we ought to give to it?

We may conclude, therefore, that in the present stage of our
history some knowledge of the future—at least, of its general
orientation—has become an urgent need in the spheres of
thought and conduct. That is why science itself is turning
more and more to this problem: " During the nineteenth
century and the early part of the twentieth, the main effort
was concentrated on illuminating mankind's *past*—and the
outcome of these investigations was in effect to demonstrate
evidentially that the appearance on earth of thought went hand
in hand, biologically speaking, with a hominization of life.
And now the moment has dawned when the light of scientific
research, *its beam turned in a forward direction*, begins to
disclose to us an even more astonishing perspective in the
extended line of the ' phenomenon of man ' : namely, a rapidly
advancing ' humanization ' of mankind."[45]

All science is to some extent focussed on the future. To a
greater or less degree the purpose of all our researches is to
equip us better for living and to give us more and more
control over coming events. As our understanding of nature
improves, so too does our ability to shape the future at will
and to foresee what is going to happen. Astronomy can
determine the position of the planets a long time in advance
and by computation predict a great many celestial phenomena.
In their study of natural forces and the properties of matter
the physicists and chemists have created an area of knowledge
which allows them to apply those forces and properties as they

wish. A doctor is able to say at once what the result of this or that course of treatment will be.

Up to a point, at least, all our scientific knowledge would be worthless if it did not have some authoritative bearing on the future. The laws of nature discovered by science apply just as much to the future as to the present and the past. The certainty that we have in this connection is not a matter of direct proof but is based wholly on an extrapolation, on our belief in the stability of nature. We cannot possibly demonstrate that Newton's law of universal attraction will still be operative to-morrow; and yet we cannot in all good reason doubt for a moment the permanent validity of that law. If we are to amass and profit from our scientific knowledge, therefore, we can only do so by postulating the stability and invariability of the laws of nature which our study of the past and present has disclosed to us.

This is every bit as true when applied to the future of cosmic evolution, which—as we have already seen—is coincident with the future of anthropogenesis. If we can succeed in discovering the fundamental laws that have governed cosmic evolution in the past, then we cannot reasonably be denied the right to project the continuing effect of those laws into the future. As our knowledge of the past increases, therefore, the more reliable our ability to foresee the further course of world evolution will become. It is in this light that we have to regard Teilhard's views about the future. Thus in a letter dated 8th September 1935 he wrote: "*The past has revealed to me how the future is built.*"[46] For him knowledge of the future was the natural—and also the most rewarding—outcome of the study of the past. All this points both to the high place to be accorded to his views regarding the future and to the fact that the basis on which they rested was indeed a scientific one.

At this juncture, however, we need to examine more precisely what his ideas on the matter were. Obviously, not every science can be made to apply to the future in the same way and with equal exactitude. In some instances it will be possible to reach almost mathematical certainty, whilst in others we must be content with more approximate knowledge. Teilhard cautions us that the latter will always be true of biological phenomena: ". . . it seems to be decidedly the case that human evolution goes beyond the bounds of exact calculation. So it would be an error, deserving of vigorous denunciation, to talk as though biology in its forecasts can behave like astronomy."[47] Does this mean that we must rest content with pure speculation and guesswork? That would be to make the opposite mistake. After citing the works of Eddington, Julian Huxley and Charles Darwin—works in which these writers deal with the future of man—Teilhard makes this observation: ". . . what surprises one on reading these various ' anticipations ' of the future, is the absence of all firm principle as a basis for the conjectures put forward. Chance gropings into the future, rather than serious *extrapolations*."[48]

Teilhard's standpoint, then, is clear. Scientific knowledge of the future is not an impossibility—on the contrary, it is in full course of realization. Mathematical certitude about this is ruled out, of course; but by making use of " serious extrapolations " we can form a reliable picture of the future. The kind of assurance that we can have in this respect lies more or less midway between the certainty which mathematics or astronomy can give us and the confidence that we can place in some guesses or conjectures. It will increase in proportion to our knowledge of the past.

Within these limits it would seem scientifically justifiable, therefore, to institute an enquiry into the future of mankind. Where is the further evolution of the world taking us; and what is to be man's part in this further development? In our thinking and our endeavours at the mundane level what is to be our goal, if we want to remain true to the deeper orientation operative in the world? The fact is that " the true summons of the Cosmos is a call consciously to share in the great work that goes on within it : it is not by drifting down the current of things that we shall be united with their one, single, soul, but by fighting our way with them, towards some Term still to come."[49]

The future will be the outcome of an interplay between the laws of nature and human freedom. Our freedom is not *in vacuo*, but is always a freedom-in-situation, as the philosophers say nowadays : a freedom within a given context. It is therefore of major importance, if man is going to build to-morrow's world, for him to know in the first place what this situation is—this context in which he will be able to fulfil a co-creative role and to co-operate in doing what he has to do.

We can see at once that any understanding of the future of man and the world in these terms has no connection with a deterministic view of history. Teilhard never envisaged the future evolution of man as an ineluctable necessity in which human freedom would have no part to play at all. On the contrary, we shall see how he calls most emphatically for man's collaboration in the process of completing cosmic evolution and sees this free collaboration as an essential factor in the course of events.[50] We are to understand his predictions, then, as having not a deterministic but only a statistical character. Just as man's behaviour may to some extent be foreseen on a basis of statistical evidence—without the voluntary character of this behaviour being thereby hindered or denied—so with our scientific knowledge of the past and of the laws contained in it as a foundation, we are able to study the future evolution of mankind. It is a future that is offered to us, not one forced ineluctably upon us.

ii *From Noosphere to Noogenesis*

It is to the past, then, that we must turn with our questioning, if we are to find out in what direction the evolutionary process is likely to move. By studying that past we learn to distinguish three main spheres in the structure of the cosmos : the sphere of matter (geosphere), the sphere of life (biosphere) and the sphere of mind (noosphere), which have been built up, historically speaking, in three sucessive phases. The last of the three to arrive is the noosphere; and as we have seen already, it is there—within the noosphere—that any further evolution is going to occur; so if we want to discover something of the structure of the future, we must first of all consider the phenomena manifested in the sphere proper to man and learn to view them in the light of those general laws which govern cosmic evolution.

If we accept in principle the idea that evolution moves on and that henceforward its point of gravity is man, it follows that we should not think of the noosphere as a static and immutable whole. Like the geosphere and the biosphere it is subject to an internal process of growth and development. We must abandon once and for all the delusion that evolution has a bearing only upon the past and that we have now reached a situation which is definitive and unchanging. No arguments for an idea of that kind really hold water. Taken as a whole, modern science leads us to one conclusion : that the cosmos is a course of events and is to be apprehended as an evolutive process on the move toward a distant future. Man is *in* evolution, " up to the neck ". Precisely because we stand right in the centre of evolution and as free and conscious beings have to do our part toward its completion, it behoves us to reflect upon the future and to have an eye to the general orientation, aim and purpose demanded of our activity. We might use a Marxist expression here and say that man must place himself within the directional movement of history and so must make it his first duty to discern what that direction is. Properly understood, the noosphere presents itself to us, therefore, as a noogenesis, as the growth-process of mind.

When we look back over man's past, we cannot escape the impression that his whole history, however uncertain and turbulent it may have been, seems nonetheless to point to a process of growth, of movement upwards, of advance. Man is a being that cannot rest on whatever has already been achieved, but on the contrary is driven by an irresistible impulse to move forward to fresh conquests.

Man is a questing, struggling, restless being. His past manifests itself to us not as a static and immutable landscape in which everything falls into its fixed and final place, but rather as a struggle, with its ups and downs, its fierce bouts of activity and periods of relative and temporary quiet, toward a vaguely sensed ideal of greater human perfection. This view of the past is in itself enough to bring home to us the large extent to which mankind is thrust forward by a force that is not to be withstood. Deep within us is the conviction that we have not as yet reached our final stage—hence the imperfection which characterizes our being. And we can only think of the future—as we do of the past—as a further ascent toward more truth and knowledge, more social justice and greater understanding, more beauty and art. It is true, of course, that we cannot exclude the possibility of a catastrophic disaster. The higher a being rises, the more vulnerable it becomes and the more exposed to danger on every side. But at all events the future cannot be seen as a standstill at the level we have reached now or as preserving unchanged the present state of affairs. Everything suggests that we should envisage the future as the continuation of a movement, of a curve, the direction and rhythm of which are already evident to us from the past.

The fundamental law which we deduced from the study of the past was that of increasing complexity and increasing consciousness. If, relying on the stability of nature's laws, we project this law into the future, it follows that we must expect an increase of complexity and consciousness in the very heart and centre of humanity itself. Thus the universal cosmic process of psychogenesis which the past reveals will continue to govern the future. Let us not, however, simply state this general thesis—even though it may appear, *a priori*, to be plausible enough—and leave it at that; but rather let us take a look at mankind to-day in its concrete situation and see whether we do not find in it symptoms tending to support our

general deduction. We shall have no trouble in establishing
that mankind to-day evinces a growing tendency to unification
and that the life of the mind—especially in the realm of
science—is all the time growing in intensity. Let us now
take a closer look at these symptoms.

Consider in the first place the symptom of unification and
its increase—glancing back for a moment to the plant and
animal world. What strikes us immediately about that is the
fact that down the centuries there has been an uninterrupted
process of progressive ramification. We find the various
species of plants and animals continually dividing and becoming more and more divergent with the passage of time. In this
way an almost infinite diversity of living beings has developed
out of a few initial types. One might at first, therefore, expect
the human tree to exemplify the same sort of thing, branching
and splintering off in a similar way. After all, do we not find
primitive man separating off into numerous races and groups,
dispersed and extended over a wide area, and having ceased for
thousands and thousands of years to have any reciprocal contact? And yet when we consider mankind to-day, the evidence
plainly points to a movement in the opposite direction. So far
from displaying symptoms indicative, biologically speaking, of
a disintegration of the human species, we find that the movement is toward a growing rapprochement and unification.
Under the influence of technics and the modern communi-
cation-media and of the stimulus afforded by trade and commerce on a world scale, the whole human race is seen to be
evolving toward a unity the like of which it has never known
before. In man the current of evolution would seem to be
suddenly changing direction and instead of making for further
differentiation, to be doing exactly the opposite by converging
toward a greater degree of unity and concentration. Quite
unexpectedly, we see the human species folding back, as it
were, upon itself and striving to realize its intrinsic oneness.[51]

For the first time in history a real unification of mankind is
beginning to take shape on a planetary scale. Now at last the
history of man, of *humanity*, would seem to be under way :

that is to say that now at last men right around the globe are beginning to sense their solidarity. All peoples and nations are faced with the same problems; and all without exception find themselves concerned with, and involved in, whatever is happening, in the same great adventure. In this development the advances made in technics have finally tipped the scale. Obviously, the tremendous expansion in the means of transport and communication, as well as of commerce and industry, has intensified contact between us and involves us in working more and more closely together. Of course, we may resist this for a time; but it cannot be long before we are obliged to give way before it. This fact—that mankind is becoming one—is by now evident to us all; but what is not generally well enough understood is the biological aspect of the development. The technical order has its roots in the biological, and in turn radically affects the course of biological evolution. In the case before us the rise of technics tells against the splintering of the human race in a biological sense—instead, its effect is to strengthen and deepen the oneness of mankind more and more.[52]

Side by side with this drawing together of all the races and peoples on earth the effort is being made to structure an interior organization. Mankind today is plainly bent on creating some organizational pattern on a planetary scale. Admittedly, we are still a long way from this goal; yet it cannot be gainsaid that men are searching and working with such an end in view and are advancing, however slowly, toward it. Along with all this go tensions and conflicts of every kind; but one has only to pierce below the surface of events to be convinced that an authentic process of organization and socialization is one of the things to which contemporary man aspires and is most deeply committed.

Thus what we perceive on the *outer* surface is an evident process of rapprochement and unification. But is not something of a similar kind happening at the deeper levels of human consciousness too? Do we not observe in the thoughts and feelings of men a process of fermentation at work, point-

ing toward greater unification? One result of contacts at the
external level is that on the mental plane also an inevitable
movement of interpenetration is taking place; and there is a
shared maturing and deepening of consciousness. It is not
merely that the various cultures are having a seminal, fructifying influence on one another, but that across every frontier
of country, race and language, there is developing a common
endeavour in the fields of science, thought, art, ethics and
— religion. In all these areas people have started to work
together; and we find such a concentration of energies and
resources as has never existed before. This is noticeable most
of all where the investigation of nature is concerned. Here a
kind of worldwide, collective mode of thinking and enquiring
has arisen, which makes it possible to tackle and solve problems
for the most part by teamwork. Research in natural science,
both as regards its programming and its results, is now an outstanding example of collective effort on the part of mankind as
a whole. But in other fields too the same sort of trend is
apparent. All thinking and enquiry assume the form of a
dialogue; and through the interchange of ideas and insights our
knowledge grows and our mental horizon is enlarged.

In the event, our sense of responsibility has been deepened
too. More than ever before, it is being brought home to us that
solidarity is an aim incumbent upon all peoples, and that the
more favoured have an obligation to help and support the
less privileged. We are coming to realize more and more
that we are all bound up together, that we constitute a great
human community and that from now on, in view of the
tremendously powerful means of extermination at our dis-
— posal, we are locked solidly together in life and death, because
we have before us only this one choice : either to live together
in peace or perish together in total disaster. In every quarter,
then—even if it is more plainly evident in some than in others
—there would seem to be symptoms pointing to a growth of
common awareness, a communal consciousness, in mankind
as a whole.

There can be no disputing the fact that these symptoms are

wholly in line with the law of increasing complexity and increasing consciousness, which we noted earlier. They tally with the general cosmic movement in which the fundamental character of biological evolution is itself disclosed to us. When we analyse the trend of events in the world today, we can only be strengthened in the conviction that the whole of mankind is on the road to increasing socialization, that we are growing out of multiplicity into unity.

The urge to socialization, to the bringing about of organic combinations, is as old as the world itself. We find it in the atoms, which build up into more and more complex structures. We find it in each line of living creatures, which in their own way strive for some form of socialization. In man the general and universal law of the cosmos is carried further.[53] In him the super-organization of matter in its onward movement is fully implemented; and as always, this movement is accompanied by a growing liberation of consciousness.[54] We must not forget that reflective thinking, however personal and inalienable it may be, always unfolds in a shared relationship with others and has an indispensable social aspect.[55]

Thus man's future, *qua* species, evidently lies in the direction of increasing socialization. But does a development of this sort not carry with it a lethal threat to the human person? Will not the whole human adventure, in that case, finally and inevitably lead to a process of " massification " in which the individual is overwhelmed in something that can only be compared to a termite colony or an antheap? This is certainly a fear that grips many of those who watch the trend of evolution in mankind to-day. And yet such a fear would seem to be ill-founded; for we must not overlook the fact that if the formation of a mass society has a depersonalizing influence, communal intercourse has precisely the opposite effect, in that it stimulates the development of personality. Real community, far from making men undifferentiated, creates diversity; and the larger and more complex the community, the more opportunity it affords each individual to develop his peculiar gifts and talents and to express his personality.

Theoretically, there are two ways of unifying mankind : by
coercion and force or by voluntary rapprochement. Coercion
and force may lead to an outward unification—but they will
never bring about an authentic, interior unanimity, an intrinsic
condition of unity. Only free and close association, only sympathy and affection, can do that. These are the truly creative
forces in the world of man, as at an inferior level and in a
weaker form they have already been the constructive forces in
the cosmos as a whole. The atoms were impelled toward one
another by an intrinsic affinity; and so the molecules came
into being. The cells coalesced; and thence the great diversity
of organisms appeared. Through the association of living
entities we get the various forms of community (the forest, the
herd, the ants' nest). Human association and union engender
the family, the nation, the community of nations. In each case
the process of coming together and of becoming united has led
to greater diversity and differentiation.

Now obviously, words like " inclination " and " love " are
used analogically here. But we ought not to be surprised at
this way of speaking. We find it already in St. Thomas
Aquinas, where he distinguishes three senses of the word
" love " : (1) in its broadest sense love can denote an attraction between two or more entities, *inclinatio rei ad aliquid*—
and so we may say that the flower loves the sun, or that certain substances are attracted by one another; (2) in a more
limited sense, however, love may signify a pleasure (found
or taken) in the good, *complacentia boni*, a " pleasure " that
is not always volitional on our part : one cannot " lay on "
sympathy to order; (3) but in its strictest and most perfect
sense love denotes a free human act whereby we will the good
of the other; then it becomes *dilectio, caritas*.

We must not quibble, therefore, over Teilhard de Chardin's
right to use the word " love " in its varying senses and to see in
love the mightiest power in the world, the power which—as
Dante says—" actuates sun and stars ". In the world of
matter and of the animals we can only speak of there being an
involuntary inclination (i.e. mutual attraction); but in the

world of men conscious love has an irreplaceable and life-giving role to play. And that community which is sustained and actuated by such love is *par excellence* the milieu in which the human person is enabled to develop to his fullest and best. So far from annihilating personality, this love affords it the greatest chance of coming to maturity.[56] We have every right, therefore, to contend that what we have called socialization presages not the end but the *beginning* of the " epoch of personality ".[57]

Thus we see evolution pursuing its course in man and, having reached this particular stage in its development, conforming to the same kind of procedure as has been employed so many times in the past, in order to bring to birth a new and still more complex form of life.

iii *The Ultimate Unity*

A careful look at the present situation of mankind against the background of evolution as a whole has taught us to recognize that we have now reached a juncture at which we are drawing closer together and becoming increasingly unified. Global solidarity, the growth in the world's population, mounting contacts under the influence of science, technics and the economic order, the unavoidable interpenetration of cultures and races—it would all seem to indicate that the cosmic organizing process is continuing apace in mankind today. The "planetization" of man has begun. We are at a moment in history when this is clearly beginning to occur. Any reversal of this movement would appear to be out of the question or would be tantamount to a disaster of catastrophic proportions.

Now the question naturally arises : to what mysterious final point must an evolutive process of this sort eventually lead? Any answer that we give can only be expressed in vague and general terms.[58] How could we describe the phases through which mankind is to pass in the further course of its evolu-

tion? How can we conceive of the organizational forms which
mankind will construct in the remote future? How can we
envisage man's psychic life over a thousand or a million years?
One thing is certain : we can only see the future as " produced " or extended along the line constituted by the past, as a
further and higher implementation of the law governing the
whole cosmic eventualizing process—the law, that is, of growing complexity and growing consciousness. As unification and
concentration intensify, mankind will be structured in a higher
form of complexity; and this higher form of complexity can
only be accompanied by a proportional consciousness, a psychic
" high tension " of unprecedented power. If the law of
complexity-consciousness operates in the future as it has in the
past—and we fail to see why that should not be the case—then
sooner or later a moment must come when mankind will have
attained to its maximal complexity and consciousness.[59]

So far as we can see it appears quite certain that the planetization of mankind will continue to advance in the direction of
a growing unification; so that we have to see the world *as a
world with a convergent structure.* Now it must surely be that
these lines of convergence will ultimately come together at a
specific point, at a centre where the whole movement merges
into one—a point which we may refer to as the point *Omega,*
the final or furthest point of the whole of biological evolution,
of the whole cosmic process : a final point where the law of
universal love will have reached its climax and its crown.

As Teilhard saw it, therefore, the future of man in all
probability lies in the social plane. The great body of mankind
must be built up out of the many cells which now lead their
separate existences. Just as the human brain consists of millions
of neurons which have been composed into a unity through
innumerable connections and combinations and thus make
possible the unitary consciousness in man, so must men combine with one another to form a kind of super-organism in
which a communal consciousness, a suprapersonal unity, would
be manifested—with this difference : that the cells which
constitute our brain no longer have an individual existence,

whereas man, in virtue of his reflective consciousness, retains his individual freedom and separate existence, even within the larger organization.[60]

So there is a fundamental difference between the hopes and expectations of a Teilhard and the picture of the future offered us by a Nietzsche. Whilst the latter, with his theory of the Superman (whether understood in a biological or an ethical sense), puts the whole emphasis on the individual man and condemns the idea of community, Teilhard on the other hand, without underestimating the value of the individual personality, sees the true completion of mankind in terms of community, of *esprit de corps* and oneness. Initially, Nietzsche too had taken a theory of evolution as his starting-point; but it goes without saying that it was very much more limited and superficial than the one to which science has led us today. Whereas Nietzsche predicted the arrival of a superman, Teilhard looked forward more to a super-mankind; and whereas Nietzsche extolled stubborn pride and egoism as supreme virtues, Teilhard's was a message of universal solidarity and love.[61]

The final term of evolution, according to Teilhard, lies in the awakening of a collective super-consciousness with its source in the moral solidarity and union of all men. To expect a thing like that may seem to us too daring and miraculous for words; but let it be borne in mind that to all normal expectation the final term can hardly be less splendid and indeed fantastic than the very process of evolution, of which it must constitute the ultimate climax and completion. Since the whole business of cosmic evolution presents an ascending line, a movement upward, then it is only reasonable to expect the apex of this movement to surpass in splendour and in value everything that comes before it.

On first impressions one might be inclined to think that Teilhard's expectation regarding the future bears a certain resemblance to Marxist ideas on the subject. Both orientate us toward an ideal community from which the contrarieties and injustices of the present will have disappeared. Yet between the two conceptions there is a crucial difference. Actu-

ally, Teilhard goes much further than does Marxism on this
score. Marxism locates the final term in a society all of whose
members have attained to a state of collective sympathy and
equality—a condition in which each individual comes to his
fulfilment and his intellectual and affective upliftedness to
the extent that he is absorbed into the larger whole. For Teilhard the completion and ultimate perfection of the human
being and of the entire community of men reside in a state
of unitive association with a super-individual and super-
personal centre. Apart from the existence of such a centre
upon which all forces converge, he holds the cohesion of a
totalized humanity to be impossible and a relapse into egoism
unavoidable.[62]

Is man going to reach this ultimate completion? That will
depend to a great extent on man himself, on his co-operation
and choice. Up to the point where man appears evolution is a
deterministic affair, following a course fixed by the laws of
nature. But with man a new phenomenon begins to come into
play within the world : the phenomenon of freedom. Thenceforward, our collaboration as free beings is required for the
continuance of the evolutive process. No longer is evolution
something which we " undergo "; we have to assume control
of it and carry it forward to its ultimate point. This consummation is offered to man : it lies within his reach, but is not
imposed, willy-nilly, upon him. In the end, therefore, it will
depend on our co-operation whether we are going to achieve
the final crown of the adventure or not.

But then the question arises as to whether man will summon
up the necessary energy and resources to travel to the end of this
road of his completion and so to reach his goal. For this two
conditions are requisite. First of all, he must be effectively
on his guard against the pessimism and despondency that might
cause him to hesitate or recoil before the effort demanded of
him. That is why all philosophies and doctrines which counsel
retreat from the world or are life-renouncing or plunge us in a
Buddhistic indifference constitute a temptation to be resisted.
It is not in isolationism or pessimism or fatalism that true

wisdom is to be found. They can lead only to our ultimate failure and undoing. The second condition is that we do precisely the reverse, by committing ourselves to evolution and its final consummation and by working for its success with all the powers at our command. To that end we must believe in man, in the world, and in our ultimate destination; we must cherish the final end in view. But is such a loving, activating and sublimating attachment feasible? Can we command sufficient love for a future centre, when that centre is envisaged as an abstraction or a " thing "? Is not all real love, in the end, focussed on a person, on a Someone? If we conceive of the point *Omega* as no more than a condition, a state, an idea, then our attachment to it will soon wither and fall away in face of the difficulties to be surmounted. If, however, we can learn to see it as a Someone, then there is a chance that love may tide us over every obstacle and that we shall find the strength to bring evolution to its final term.

Men's task—their great task as free and intelligent beings— consists in the noble enterprise of bringing the cosmos to its completion; and to this we are incited not only by the dynamic of evolution—which, as Bergson showed, is a *vis a tergo*, impelling us forward—but even more by the attractive force exerted by the ultimate end itself which—*ab ante*, as it were— is pulling the whole cosmos in its direction. We are born and we live in the function of a cosmic movement. Our existence as individuals is dependent on, and subject to, a universal destiny, within which each of us must fulfil his appointed task and assume his allotted place.

iv *Retrospect*

There is a famous portrait of Descartes, painted by the Dutch artist Weenix, which depicts the father of modern philosophy holding a book on which are inscribed these words: *Mundus est fabula*, the world is a tale. There has been a good deal of discussion about what these words may have meant to Descartes.

It would seem to us that they would not be out of place,
however, beneath a photograph of Teilhard : for him too the
world was a meaningful tale, a " history"—but in quite a
different sense, of course, from anything that Descartes may
have meant by that phrase.

The cosmos is a spatio-temporal unity which discloses its
inner structure and deeper meaning only when we come to
analyse its evolutionary history and lay bare the "inside
works" determining the course which that history has taken.
In its deepest essence the world, in Teilhard's view, is a psychic
kind of a thing : "a huge psychic phenomenon",[63] an ascent
toward more and more perfect consciousness, based on ever
more complex structures. This movement of the entire cosmos
in the direction of consciousness is most plainly evident in biological evolution which, although only subsidiary, only a
constituent, is nevertheless the most important and most
revealing part of the whole.[64] This biological evolution has
resulted in man; so we may justifiably say that in him the
world's nature is revealed at its deepest level : ". . . the story
of life is no more than a movement of consciousness veiled by
morphology."[65] Teilhard was certainly not the first to stress
in this way the psychic element in the structure of the universe.
It is a notion entertained by many thinkers, from Spinoza to
Heymans. With most of them, however, it was the outcome
of philosophical reflection and was connected with their particular theory of knowledge and their metaphysics. Teilhard's
starting-point is quite different. It is simply and solely that of
the natural scientist—although the conclusions which he drew
no doubt go beyond the experimental facts. His purpose was
" to co-ordinate and organize the lines of the world".[66] He
called this new type of science a phenomenology, because it is
meant to abstract as thoroughly as possible every philosophical
and theological method in order to leave the field quite clear
for the phenomenal evidences provided by natural science—
with the proviso that these phenomena be interpreted not
simply in their sheer facticity but also in terms of their

inner orientation and their organic connection with the whole.

Undoubtedly, a salient feature of the picture which Teilhard thereby presented of the world is its closely knit internal coherence. What apparently gave it birth was a single initial intuition, which came to him at an early stage and attained greater depth and outreach as the years passed and as Teilhard tested it against his experience. He detected in the cosmos as a whole an awe-inspiring and thoroughgoing coherence, a profound organizational unity in which everything is bound up with everything else and takes its *raison d'être* from its place within the whole.[67]

We said just now that Teilhard's world view presents itself as a " phenomenology " and not as in any sense a philosophical or theological construction. That does not mean, of course, that it has no need to be supplemented and elucidated by those disciplines. It resolves none of the ultimate questions regarding the cosmos in which we live and the purpose or meaning of this world and of man's existence in it. What it does is to provide a substructure which philosophy and theology must reckon with. An enquiry in greater depth into the origin of the cosmos and the nature of psychism—especially in the case of man—is therefore still the reserve of those disciplines.

Let us take Teilhard's work for what it is—something with definite limitations, and yet something of impressive depth and richness too. There can be no doubt that on its own ground it represents one of the most masterly attempts so far made to harness the insights of the natural sciences as they are today, in order to come at a sound and justifiable notion of the cosmos and its inner structure.

That notion is based principally on the evolutive aspect of the universe. For Teilhard the world is first and foremost a history; and this way of history seems to him the only possible way by which to arrive at an understanding, a concept, of the world. In that respect his work is consonant, up to a point, with Marxism, which likewise puts a special emphasis on the historical aspect of things. On the Catholic side some have chosen to take offence at this—wrongly, as we think. A Christian view of things, properly understood, is equally bound to allow a fundamental place to the historical aspect presented by the world, since according to that view God is himself manifested in and through history[68] and it is through the course of history that the " Mystical Body " is to be built up. Within the Christian perspective too the world is a history which faith invests with yet other dimensions on a supernatural plane, so that the message of salvation is as it were wrapped in the vesture of a " holy ", a " sacred ", history.

We would be doing less than justice, however, to the world view formulated by Teilhard, if we were to think of it only as a conception of the cosmos which is grounded in science, coheres in harmonious fashion and is firmly anchored in history. It really involves much more than that. It is also meant to give an orientation to our conduct, to be an invitation to man to co-operate in realizing the great end that must be reached. It directs our gaze to the future and fills our hearts with hope and expectation. The world that we live in is a world in which we have a task to fulfil, a world which we are in duty bound to carry forward to its completion. It is more than a fortuitous and ephemeral stop upon our way : it is a testing and a task, is part and parcel of our very selves. Man's place in this world is not that of an accidental, inexplicable, marginal phenomenon. He is no stranger or sojourner here. Indeed, it is in him that the whole value and significance of the cosmos is vested and expressed; and it is his task to bring it to its ultimate goal.[69]

Mankind today is still only in its primary stage. Measured by the standards of evolution, a few thousand centuries are only a brief span of time. There is every reasonable prospect that many thousands, perhaps millions, of years still lie ahead for mankind. The imperfect conditions which obtain now are no reason for discouragement or despair. We must keep steadily in view the ultimate goal—a purpose surely impressive and inspiring enough—and bend all our energies to the job of bringing it nearer. Our efforts to advance science, to develop technics, commerce and industry, to revitalize philosophy and the arts, to plan the present and future of society and bring order into international affairs—all that has its place in this great enterprise, is invested by it with profounder meaning, with a loftier spirit of consecration. But above all it is our task in this world to promote and foster concord, unity and love. These are the great constructive forces of the future. The future of mankind—and thus of the whole evolutionary process—stands or falls by the amount of love that we are going to be able to command.

Teilhard's vision of the world is charged, therefore, with a deeper undertone of optimism; and in this it contrasts sharply with the sombre and pessimistic ideas propounded in recent years by certain philosophers and other writers. His message is one of hope and confidence. We learn from him not of anguish and nausea but of love—love of life and love for the world: not of "aloneness" but of union. Arnold Toynbee had good reason, therefore, to describe *The Phenomenon of Man* as "an act of spiritual liberation".[70] In his brilliant study of Jean-Paul Sartre, R.-M. Albérès shows that what constitutes the central problem for this philosopher is the human being's responsibility for his destiny. But, he adds, "in M. Sartre we find nothing of a cosmic sense, no echo resonant of the human adventure, certainly no Faith. Man is imprisoned in human consciousness, having no bond of kinship with the earth, with nature, with the cosmos".[71] Undoubtedly, the comment is a fair one. We are at once aware of the gulf that there is between Sartre and Teilhard. For Sartre man is entirely isolated from the world around him and thrown back onto himself. With Teilhard, however, man has a sense of being intimately linked with the whole cosmic process of evolution and is invited to rise out of and above himself in shouldering a glorious task.

In *Thus Spake Zarathustra* Nietzsche has his prophet address these words to the people: "I adjure you, brothers, always be faithful to the earth." Teilhard also speaks to us of a fidelity

to the earth.[72] But how utterly different for him is the impli-
cation of those words! The fidelity to the earth which he
enunciated is a " fidelity " to the mighty work proceeding in
the cosmos—an ascent to mind and spirit, a consummation
through love and union, a collective movement toward the
suprapersonal centre on which the whole of evolution con-
verges.

PART II

A religion with a
Christological structure

Chapter 4

RELIGION EARTHLY AND
RELIGION HEAVENLY

The central problem with which Teilhard wrestled throughout his life was—as we said at the outset of this study—the question of the relation between God and the universe.

If this problem were to be resolved, what was required before anything else was a thorough study of the cosmic phenomenon; and the results of that study we have tried to present in the foregoing pages. We have to learn to see the cosmos as an organically evolving whole, the inner orientation of which is centred on the emergence and upward movement of mind; so that cosmogenesis is to be envisaged in the final instance as a noogenesis. At the very heart of that noogenesis there is now manifested a movement of convergence, which ultimately is bound to debauch in a spiritual centre of a problem as stated. If a lot of people get hold of the idea that the efforts of mankind at large ought to be directed.

This, however, is but a first step toward a solution of the problem as stated. If a lot of people get hold of the idea that the whole of Teilhard's work must be comprised under his scientific phenomenology, that must be ascribed to the fact that a great part of his writings—specifically, those relating to the religious issue—have not yet been published. Actually, the religious problems have a very big place in his posthumous writings. He always was preoccupied with the religious issues more even than with the purely scientific ones. For him the divide between the two worlds was a psychological impossibility. To concern oneself only with science and simply to

111

thrust aside philosophical and theological issues—this he
described as "a psychologically untenable situation". All
scientific work must, in the final instance, be supported
and stimulated by some kind of "faith".[1]

Throughout his life, therefore, he was constantly confronting his scientific insights with his religious convictions; and
his purpose in so doing was not just to obviate any possible
conflict between the two, but also to achieve a vital synthesis
between them.

This was in the first place a matter of satisfying a personal
mental requirement, a matter of an inner experience to which
he wanted to testify. It was his deepest conviction that he was
really no exception in this and that many people in our day,
within the Christian fold as well as outside it, have had to
struggle with the same sort of problem. That is why he considered it a duty to impart the results of his personal questing
to others, in the hope that they might be of some benefit to
such people in their personal difficulties : " I am very much
aware," he wrote to a young friend, "that I am just a sound-
ing-board which reflects—only more strongly—what others
around me are thinking. I neither am nor wish to be a pre-
ceptor. Take from me what you please, and build your own
structure."[2]

His theological views he regarded only as : "suggestions,
not assertions or tenets".[3]

Let us, then, take a look at his ideas in just the way that he
himself intended.

i *The New World View and the Modern Religious Sense*

The mental outlook of people to-day is governed predomin-
antly by the natural sciences and the view of the world which
they have engendered. Contemplating the world as it now
presents itself to us has turned the spotlight on to two discoveries : " two essential discoveries which have produced, and
continue to permeate the modern mentality a) the discovery,

first, of the structurally linked immensity of space, which imbues our accustomed way of looking at things with a strain of *Universalism* b) secondly, the discovery of the structurally linked (and progressive) *Duration of time* which in turn introduces into our accustomed perspectives the idea of a possible unlimited Progress (Futurism) . . . Universalism and Futurism, conjoined in our perception of a universe in global growth (Evolution). In itself, the appearance of these two new characteristics is a great psychological event. Not only do they impart two dimensions to our experience. . . but what is more, they also express a *religion*, since (by definition) the religious appears as soon as the world is viewed in its totality and in terms of its future consummation (Faith)."[4]

This assessment is most important. It is undeniable that the notion we form of the universe affects the whole of our interior life and also our religious sense. F. Gonseth is right when he says : " Just as the heavens dominate and environ the earth on every side, so the consciousness of man is always dominated and enveloped by some sort of cosomogenic doctrine."[5] We have become aware of the gigantic dimensions and organic cohesion of the universe. Out of this new way of feeling and conceiving the cosmos a new form of natural religion—or religiousness—has emerged which is focussed completely on the earth and its trans-historical consummation. The world has become for us " an object of superior worth and dignity to which we owe an evident debt of submission and dedication. Through the undeniable attraction exerted by a close and palpable immensity we feel a demand made upon our natural inclination to worship . . . within a few generations mankind has been literally and spontaneously converted to a kind of religion of the world, vague in its dogmas yet perfectly clear in its moral orientations. These are : the acknowledged predominance of the totality over the individual; a passionate belief in the worth and potentialities of human endeavour; a lively awareness of the sacred nature of scientific enquiry *in all fields*. Just because science has discovered the natural unity of the world—and just how vast it is—modern man can no longer see God, save in the prolongation (perhaps one might say : under the aspect) of a universal progress or maturation."⁶

In the eyes of men today this belief in mundane values and in progress finds its justification in the new perspectives that science has attained vis-à-vis the structure of the universe and the historical character of human existence. It is well aware of the backing it enjoys from the enormous advances made by technics and the hopes for the future that such progress arouses. Man has come to realize what his task is in this world and what his responsibility is towards the future. From now on his life is sustained and inspired " by the faith and hope in some salvation bound up with the consummation of the earth ".⁷

This is not to say that contemporary man is a-religious. We are nearer the truth if we say that the religious sense present in every individual has assumed another form, a new orientation : " Say what we will, our century is religious—perhaps more so than any other . . . Only it has not yet found the God whom it can worship "⁸ . . . " We might say that a new, until now unprecedented, form of religion (a religion that no one has yet been able to visualize or describe, because a vision of the universe big enough and organic enough to serve as a basis for it has been wanting) is germinating in the heart of man today— and is doing so in the trail blazed by the idea of evolution."⁹

Ever since the Renaissance this natural religiousness, this form of faith and veneration, has been gradually gaining mastery over the soul of man. It has broadened out and intensified over the years, as scientific investigation has made clear, to more and more stupendous effect, the size and nature of the universe and has brought home to us just how much mankind may be able to achieve in the way of furthering the progress of this world of ours. Our whole modern attitude to life turns fundamentally upon this sense that we are responsible for the world; and it is this that lies at the root of what has come to be called " modern atheism ". Very little indeed separates such atheism from the religion of earth. No one has put this better than Jean Lacroix : " Modern man often has the feeling that by means of science and technology together he is able, as it were, to improve upon nature, that is to say, by contributing in some sense to her development and growth process, to alter, so to speak, the history of nature and the history of man. He simply feels sorry for the fear-ridden, for those who decline to take in hand the lot of the world and the destiny of man. Seen in this way, scientific atheism ceases to be purely systematic and becomes a sort of humanism. The atheist then becomes a person whose endeavour it is to shoulder responsibility for the world and for mankind and to apply the only means suited to that end. Atheism then presents itself as a readiness to shoulder man's responsibilities to the full."[10] It is precisely because of this stress which atheism puts on human responsibility toward the world and the human race that so many minds—and those by no means the worst—are powerfully attracted by it. " Atheism . . . is not so much out to disprove the existence of God as to give man a hold upon his own existence."[11]

From this cult of the earth and the vital task which it presents a new humanism has been born, a humanism that has its centre of gravity in the historical character of man's being. We are the upholders and creators of history. Our energies should be concentrated on building a better and juster world, where man can come to full maturity. " So the awareness of our historicity would appear to be the motor, the force actuating mankind at this present juncture; and it is just that which gives contemporary humanism not only a particular colour but also an extraordinary degree of vitality."[12]

Teilhard was keenly sensitive to this orientation of feeling and outlook on life to-day; and his diagnosis tallied closely with those of the best observers of the modern mentality. The fact that we are becoming aware of our freedom and our responsibility toward the future is in his view—despite the delusions and mistakes into which it may lead us—a valuable, definitive achievement of contemporary thinking. The lucid aversion to fatalism, to a passive suffrance of life, is perhaps one of the most important things to have transpired within the frame of mind of men to-day—something with which every world view, every philosophy, every religion must from now on come to terms. The will to improve the world with the aid of more science, more technics, better organization of its economic and social life—more culture too—represents in contemporary man the most radical force stimulating and actuating his life.

But what Teilhard did more than others was to drive home the intrinsic connection between this modern mentality and the cosmological insights of present-day science. It corresponds in some measure to the present phase of noogenesis—one in which man has come to realize that it is his job consciously to bring evolution further on toward its completion. Previously, we "underwent" evolution, in a passive sense; but now we have entered upon the epoch of self-evolution. And since we live in an evolving world which exhibits a convergent character, we are in duty bound to concentrate our efforts on this new form of life together in a society where justice, *esprit de corps* and a better spiritual and intellectual life will be realized.

It is no coincidence, therefore, that ours is the time when contemporary thought in both philosophy and religion is focussed on the theme of human freedom and responsibility.

ii *The Modern Religious Sense and Christianity*

Between this earth-centred religion and Christianity there is a sharp contrast which at first sight would appear to be insuperable. Admittedly, both forms of "religiousness" are marked by "universalism and futurism"; but the meaning covered by these terms is not always the same. "By reason of their origin the universalism and futurism of the modern world exhibit a pantheistic, immanent, organicist and evolutive character . . . whereas in Christianity they go hand in hand with concepts such as personality, transcendence, juridical relations, a doctrine of fixity."[13]

In Teilhard's opinion it is here that the real nub of the conflict dividing the two outlooks on life is to be found. " The real struggle going on around us is not between believers and unbelievers, but between two categories of believers. Two conceptions, two ways of envisaging the divine, stand face to face. The best (and so the most formidable) of the anti-Christians keep away from Christianity, not because it is too hard for them but because it appears to them not sufficiently exalted. If they do not accept Christ, it is because they do not detect in him the features which they reverence and look for. An earth-centred religion is beginning to pit itself against the heavenly one. That is the real situation—in all its gravity, yet also in its hopeful aspect."[14]

What impression does Christianity make on modern man : that is, on men who have become aware of the real dimensions of the universe and of the creative function which it is ours to fulfil in this world? Must not this contemporary man feel that Christians are still for the most part " the odd men out ", that they fail to comprehend the psychological revolution which has taken place? Many Christians persist in refusing to accept the new perspectives about which not a single scientist—outside of these Christian circles—entertains a momentary doubt; and if they do sometimes go along with these things, it is not with the openness and enthusiasm which others bring to such ideas. Instead of being cheered by what human effort has been able to accomplish, they appear to find a hidden pleasure in drawing attention to the shortcomings and imperfections that still occur and in minimizing the hopes and expectations of men. What consecration and enrichment of our human endeavours can we look for in that direction? Only with much hesitation and great reluctance will they participate in the struggle for progress which engages and motivates the best minds in the world of today. However wrong and one-sided it may be, this *is* the impression that many non-Christians get from watching the behaviour of Christians.[15] " How is it possible that nine times out of ten your believing Christian is at the human level a sceptic . . . This is what the Gentiles find so shocking. . . ."[16] Teilhard never ceased to deplore this attitude, which he considered to be at the root of the crisis besetting Christianity to-day. " What is Christian and what is human no longer appear to coincide. Hence the great schism that threatens the Church."[17] Hence too the opposition between faith in God and faith in the world.

Of course, that is not the only criticism brought by the opponents of Christianity against religion. Teilhard never set out to offer a complete diagnosis of the evolution of religion in the world. But his many contacts with unbelievers—and he spent the greater part of his life among such people—persuaded him that the attitude taken by many Christians to the new scientific world view and to the efforts being made to achieve progress and make new conquests in the social and cultural sphere was one of the chief causes of modern unbelief. " In search of a name for the unknown God of their surmising, the pagans look at us. And having done so, they recoil from a gospel that does not seem to answer to the perspectives in which they see the world or to their questions or to their expectations. The resistance to her expansion which the Church encounters at the present time is not, as is sometimes said, connected with the fact that her dogmas are too sublime and her system of morality too hard, but is owing rather to the fact that people no longer recognize in us their religious and moral ideal and so turn away in the hope of finding something better."[18]

Yet the opposition between this " new religion " and Christianity is not felt only among non-Christians. It is present in the hearts and minds of many Christians too; for they also feel inwardly torn apart, they experience a sort of " religious schizophrenia ".[19] They sense that in the very heart and centre of our modern civilization a totally new conception of the world and of man has gradually but irresistibly made its way. The humanism of earlier centuries, the humanism of a well ordered world and of "harmonious man", has been superseded. "In its place—and under the irresistible pressure of co-reflection—there is developing more or less everywhere a new Humanism: not a Humanism of equilibrium but a Humanism of movement, a Humanism which cannot feel at home with any sort of value—least of all on the score of religion—unless it leaves room for an ultra-human cosmic future and unless the claims of *that* are taken into account."[20]

Yet on the other hand this new feeling about life has not so far been integrated with the Christian vision of the world. The tenets of Christianity continue to be expressed in formulas which took their origin from, and have been very considerably influenced by, ideas belonging to a by-gone period. As a result of this there is a discordant element in the life and faith of many Christians, a malaise urgently needing to be overcome, if that faith is to be lived out at full strength and with unimpaired intensity. Even from a purely Christian standpoint, therefore, a new confrontation is called for between the age-old verities of Christianity and the mental climate prevailing among people to-day.

iii *The Threefold Task of Present-Day Theology*

Teilhard was always wanting theology to attend to this confrontation between Christianity and the modern religious sense. That was the sole purpose of the many articles which he devoted to this subject. In the meantime, without wishing in any way to take over the job of the professional theologian, he set out to find a solution to the problem for himself and for those who sought his advice. We should always bear in mind the standpoint that he adopted in so doing. His orthodoxy is not to be doubted for a moment. His love for Christ and the Church are above and beyond all questioning.[21] In

his early days he had had sufficient theological training to
know what is required of the Catholic intellectual who wishes
to examine the whys and wherefores of his faith.

The renewal at which he aimed in theology never affected
the kernel of Catholic teaching in matters of faith, but only its
exterior aspect, the way in which it was presented. He believed
that the solution and the renewal which was so badly needed
were to be found not in a departure from traditional theology
but in a deeper exploration of it.

This necessary renewal and exploration in depth had to do
primarily with three things. The first demand that he made
of theological thinking in our time concerned the new perspectives reached by science. To his mind the theologians were
not taking enough notice of the results obtained by modern
science and of the new picture of the world which they disclosed. That Teilhard was not alone in holding this view is
evident from an address given by Cardinal Cushing, Arch-
bishop of Boston. In a speech made on the occasion of the
five-hundredth anniversary of the death of Prince Henry the
Navigator the Cardinal declared that theologians "tilt at all
sorts of windmills, but have not paid sufficient attention to the
difficult problems that keep science and faith apart. . . . If
the man of science has not seldom underestimated the place of
religion in human life, it is also true that all too often the theologian has himself been ignorant with regard to the achieve-
ments of science and unfamiliar with the hazards of scientific
investigation. Far too many theologians write and preach
about subjects which have long ceased to be relevant or have
only a very remote bearing on the problem of life today."[22]
It is a fact not open to dispute that Catholic theology came into
existence at a period when the ideas that people had about the
universe were still extremely narrow and defective. For the
Church Fathers of antiquity as also for the great medieval
thinkers it was the Greek notion of the world that was in
the background of their minds and of their intellective life.

This extremely " cribbed " and static picture undoubtedly had an influence on the way in which they interpreted and gave formal expression to some of the dogmas of Christianity. Again, some perspectives that were implicit in revealed doctrine were not as yet accessible to the human mind and intellect, because the background needed for them to become conceivable was not yet there. When with the Renaissance the old world view started to break up and new insights regarding the structure of the universe gradually emerged, people largely failed to realize how important for theology this event was going to be—as was again the case in the nineteenth century, when new ideas about biological evolution came to the fore. There were many instances where certain theologians, despite an insufficient knowledge of the scientific data, even felt obliged, in the name of this or that outmoded thesis of mediaeval philosophy or theology, to take issue with specific scientific theories.

This was so especially in the area of the theory of biological evolution. Although there were great minds—one thinks, for instance, of Cardinal Newman—who perceived straightaway the rightness of the evolutionist principle,[23] the majority of theologians long refused to accept the consequences of this theory, whilst others who did their utmost to reconcile the theory of evolution with Christianity found as a result that ecclesiastical sanctions were applied against them. Those times are now past; and it is one of the most important services performed by Teilhard that he contributed in large measure to a better understanding of the problem. Nowadays the principle of evolutionism is generally accepted among Catholics, although there are still some theologians who fail to reckon sufficiently with the implications of the new world view. In Teilhard's opinion their reservations on this score do nothing but harm to the cause of religion; and the fear which they entertain regarding certain tenets is really devoid of any foundation.

This does not mean that the Church ought to tie her doctrine to a particular theory in natural science. It is not her business to stand surety for this or that way of envisaging the universe. What Teilhard desiderates is not that theologians should espouse and propagate a particular world system as a hard-and-fast doctrine—that would be too stupid for words—but simply that theology remain true to a centuries-old tradition by expressing Christian doctrine in a language likely to be understood by men and women of to-day. St. Augustine proclaimed the Christian revelation in the language of his century, against a background of the Platonism prevailing at that time. St. Thomas Aquinas formulated the dogmas of Christianity within a framework of the resurgent Aristotelean science and philosophy. In each century theology has known how to talk the language required to enable her message to be understood. Her task now is to find a language, a form of expression, a way of presenting things, that will make sense to the people of this generation. Jean Guitton writes in his Journal : " It was a great mistake to create the impression that the Incarnation of God's Son was somehow indissolubly connected with the idea of an immobile earth. It would be just as big a mistake to want to establish a necessary connection between Christianity and a vague theory of evolution."[24] In a sense he is right. But we would just like to add this : in earlier centuries the only way in which theologians *could* think of and represent God's becoming man was within the framework of a static view of the world. Now that it is evident to every thinking person that we live in an organically evolving world, the believer *can* only conceive of the Incarnation in the setting of this new world view. If Jean Guitton wants us to give an account of the Incarnation without the concrete world as background, then he is asking the impossible. At all events our proclamation of the faith has got to be cut loose from an outmoded world view—which, alas, is not yet altogether the case.

Dr. A. Hulsbosch is right, therefore, when in his genuinely trail-blazing work, *De Schepping Gods*, he says : " If preaching is to be effective, it is absolutely essential that the congregation should have it expressed in terms of their whole world of ideas. Preaching is not possible if it is divorced from whatever world view is current at the time. Proclamation lacking such a view—or tied to what is left of an old one—will be abstract or nonsensical for those who hear it."[25]

Understood in this way, Teilhard is entirely right and wholly in line with the tradition of theology when he asks the theologians to-day to be willing to face up to this new state of affairs. His *second* stipulation is consequently that the Catholic dogmas—the unchanging character of which is a matter of certainty for every believer—should be confronted with the picture that modern science presents of the world and with that sense of religion which is a product of it. It is not enough to affirm that there is no conflict, no incompatibility, between the dogmas of Christianity and the perspectives of contemporary science. The important thing is to show how the two terms may be brought together *concretely*, and a harmonious relation established between them.

His aim is clear enough, therefore. What he wants is for Catholic doctrine, which until now has always been formulated within the framework of a static view of the world, to be stated from now on in the setting of a world conceived in dynamic terms. A measure of transposition is necessary here, " the transposition into cosmogenic dimensions of the traditional view expressed in cosmic terms : creation, spirit, evil, God (and, more specifically, original sin, the cross, the resurrection, the parousia, charity . . .)—all these notions, once they are transposed to a ' genesis' dimension, become amazingly clear and coherent."[26] He is convinced that " the most traditional Christianity . . . can be interpreted so as to embrace all that is best in the aspirations peculiar to our times."[27] To make this evident is the job of the theologian who has understood what the spiritual predicament of our time is. " The reconciliation at a practical level of the natural and the supernatural in a single, harmonious orientation of human activity—here is a problem a thousand times more acute than all the theoretical difficulties that one can rake together on the question of the essential nature of grace."[28]

The central problem in this confrontation is undoubtedly that of the relation between God and the world. Teilhard asks us, therefore, to give our utmost attention to it : " In every branch of sacred science, the time has come to investigate, by study and by prayer, the area in which God and the Cosmos come together."[29] Especially now that the world has acquired a totally new prospect and man has become aware of the challenge and the task before him, it is of paramount importance for the religious life of mankind that we should concentrate our attention on this issue. The point of contact, however, between God and the world is located, for the Christian, in the person of the God-man. Hence the necessity for us to give profounder consideration to Christology and especially to examine, in the sources of Revelation, the place occupied by Christ in the divine plan and purpose for the world. Is it not strange—Teilhard asks—that in contrast to Mariology, Christology during the last few centuries has, so to speak, ceased to make any further progress? In this field there has been no advance beyond the definitions drawn up in the earliest centuries of the Church—as though these will have said all there is to say about " the unfathomable riches of Christ ".[30] It is just this relation of Christ to the world, therefore, that is to become the principal theme in Teilhard's theological reflection; and it should be said that in this he is in full rapport, as we shall see in more detail, with one of the most ancient and most splendid currents of theological thinking.

The *third* request that he makes of present-day theology has to do more with " ethos " or, if you will, with a renewal of Christian spirituality. As we said before, the problem of the relation between the world and God is *par excellence* a practical one. Whatever his theoretical reflections may be, their primary purpose is to give an orientation to human conduct— an orientation in which science and faith encounter each other and in which the things of earth and the things of heaven, which are man's occupation and concern, may discover their essential unity. Nothing is so important as to imbue man's activity with its true quality of purposiveness and at the same time to encourage the utmost exertion of his powers.

What it amounts to—to put it concretely—is that he is asking us to pay more attention to the business of thinking theologically about what has been called "mundane reality". What value does revelation attach to human toil and to man's life on this earth? Is this world, for the Christian, just a kind of transit-camp, an antechamber to eternity, or does it also represent a challenge, a task and a vocation? Do the many forms of human activity—whether in the field of science and of art or in those of technics, economics, politics, the duties of the home, and so forth—possess an intrinsic value, an intrinsic orientation with a religious significance? Is it at all possible to reconcile the gospel teaching about detachment and self-denial on the one hand with, on the other, the love of earthly things and the effort required to build a better world?

These and many other questions arise here for the Christian who is conscious of his situation in this world of ours and is seeking a firm guiding principle for his inner life. What it comes to in the end is the old problem of Christian humanism, which aspires to an "incarnational Christianity" and tries to assimilate cultural and social values to the Christian vision of the world.

Those, then, are the three main demands that Teilhard makes of modern theology : to have an attitude of openness toward the results and current perspectives of the natural sciences, to make the effort to transpose the dogmas of Christianity into the framework of the new picture that we have of the world, and to ponder seriously on the religious value of human endeavour in the temporal plane. In making this threefold demand he does not stand alone. A great deal of what has been written by theologians in recent years shows that on each score this concern is very much a part of the life and thought of Christendom at the present time. A lot of Catholics— priests as well as laity—are asking themselves the same kind of questions. Teilhard knew very well that he was voicing the concern of a great number of people; and it was this that led him to press insistently for a deeper investigation of these problems.

Understood in broad terms, these three principles or *desiderata* are not open to serious objection. It is obvious by now that theological thinking in our age has got to make a critical appraisal of its position, of precisely where it stands with regard to the possibilities and prospects now opened up by science. The best among our contemporary theologians are fully conscious of all this, although there is still no shortage of places where the importance of these issues has so far failed to penetrate. It is for that very reason that the life and work of Teilhard have served to meet a real and urgent need. His considerable scientific attainments and his familiarity with the mind and temper of our day gave him the right to speak; and we appreciate that he felt himself in duty bound to make his voice heard even on such matters as these.[31] His aim was not to construct an original "theology", but merely to provide some bricks which in his view could be of use for the new construction and without which no adequate theology was in future going to be possible.

Chapter 5

COSMOLOGY AND CHRISTOLOGY

In his writings Teilhard approaches Christianity from two different directions. On the one hand he sets himself the task of studying and analysing it as a purely historical phenomenon, with a view to laying bare its typical properties and structures, so that he can then compare these with the fundamental characteristics and requirements of a world in process of convergent evolution. On the other hand we come across pages in his writings which ought to be included under the heading of theology.

The distinction between a phenomenological approach to Christianity and a theological one is most important. Anyone who loses sight of the distinction runs the risk of misinterpreting Teilhard's ideas in this field or of setting them in a false light—and that must inevitably give occasion for all sorts of misunderstandings. In his phenomenological analyses of Christianity Teilhard views that religion simply and solely as a phenomenon alongside other phenomena, as a historical fact and nothing more. He aims to bring out as sharply as he can the essential features of Christianity and its spiritual structure and thus to set its contours clearly over against those of other major world religions. What he understands by Christianity, considered as a phenomenon, is the experimental subsistence, in and amid the human race, of a religious current marked by an intense vitality, by a remarkable capacity for adaptation which makes it (in contrast to other religions) amenable to inner renewal and growth, and finally by the striking affinity between its dogmatic perspectives (a convergence of the universe upon a self-subsistent and suprapersonal God) and everything that we learn from studying the phenomenon of man.[32]

Leaving aside the belief in a personal God, Christianity comprises the following elements : 1) in this religion a person, the person of Christ, occupies a central place. He is not only its founder (other religions too have a founder) or a message-bearer; he is himself the actual content of his message. One becomes a Christian not by assenting to this or that doctrine or by practising a certain code of morals, but in the first place by being united with Him, or as Paul says, by being " incorporated " into Him; 2) this person has said that he will return at the end of the Age—and this return forms the crowning point and consummation of world history. Christianity bids us look not to the past but to the future and to the completion of world; 3) the return of Christ must be prepared for by the gradual building up of the Mystical Body, that is, the unification of all men around and in Christ—for the total Christ consists of the Head *and* the members. All things are to be brought into unity under the one Head, Christ (*recapitulare omnia in Christo*; Eph. 1.9-10), so that the whole world is made the " pleroma " (fullness, the completion of Christ; 4) the ethics of Christianity is summed up in the commandment to love our neighbour. The Christian is not to content himself with doing no evil, no harm to his fellow man (a passive sort of neighbourly love), but must make it his business to do good with all the powers at his command and to further the happiness, the well-being of other people (an active love of one's neighbour).

All these elements are essential parts of Christianity and form the authentic nucleus of it. If we now compare them with the structural properties of an evolving world such as we know this one to be, it is easy enough to see to what a great extent this religion harmonizes with such a world, giving it a sublime centre and a fundamental law, and answering in full to its deepest needs and expectations. Far from appearing as a heterogeneous element, it stands out on the contrary as a natural complement, a natural completion, of this world. If one wanted to devise a religion that would fall within the extended line of general evolution, one would be hard put to it to think up anything better than this or anything that would be more in harmony with the world in which we live.

By pursuing this line of reasoning at greater depth we are able to perceive " a harmony of a higher order ", the beauty and extraordinary magnitude of which Teilhard never wearied of proclaiming. This harmony between the deeper structure of Christianity and the requirements of a convergent evolution represented for him a rational justification of his faith and was for him " the miracle *par excellence* ".[33] Is not harmony indeed the peculiar attribute of truth?

None of this has so far anything to do, of course, with a theology as such. At most, what one could perhaps find in these ideas would be a point of departure for an apologetics suited to the mental outlook of modern man. The theological assessment can only begin when in the light of faith the Christian comes to examine more profoundly the content and purport of revelation. The theological problems that Teilhard broached in any detail are rather few and far between. We said earlier on that it was never his intention to develop a comprehensive " theology ". Many of the essential themes of Christian doctrine are touched on only in passing, some are developed rather more, others again are not so much as mentioned. It would be a gross mistake to want to attach some special significance either to his silences or to his purely accidental references. They simply did not happen to lie within the complex of problems that engaged his attention in the religious field.

There is one problem, however, on which he focussed his attention and with which he remained concerned throughout his life—a problem to which he devoted much consideration and comment and to which he constantly returns in his religious writings. It has to do with the place and function assumed and fulfilled by Christ in the whole of cosmic history. Strictly speaking, this is no new problem. The question of the place which Christ occupies in the world is as old as Christianity

itself. The early Fathers of the Church, and the theologians of
later periods, made it their business to formulate as accurately
as they could the relation between Christ and the world and to
define precisely in what way he is connected with the history
of mankind, with the past and with the future. Even so, the
world which they had in view was a static world, the intrinsic
cohesion of which they were in no position to guess at. The
question that they posed, therefore, was as to the place of Christ
within the static and constricted world of their day.

For Teilhard this problem necessarily assumed another
aspect, in view of the revolution that had occurred in our
manner of envisaging the world. We live in an evolving
world with a convergent structure; so that when the theologian
is faced with the question of what place Christ occupies in the
world as a whole, he is obliged to take this new world view
into account. Is there any link between the God-man and this
evolving world; and if there is, is it to be construed as a
merely external, juridical connection, or ought we to think of it
rather as a close, organic relatedness? If Teilhard's contribution was original, it is because he stated the old problem of
the place of Christ in God's plan for the world in a new way.

i *Earlier Conceptions*

But if we are to get a good grasp of his ideas on this score, we
must cast our minds back for a moment to the way in which
previous ages offered to solve the problem. Strictly speaking,
no clear and generally agreed solution had hitherto been found.
People since the Middle Ages, meditating on the meaning of
the Incarnation, had arrived at two different conceptions of it
—usually referred to as the Thomist and Scotist theories—
which despite a great deal that they had in common nevertheless parted company on an important point.

According to the Thomist view of the matter,[34] a rigid
distinction must be drawn between the order of creation and
the order of redemption. In the original plan for the world

(the order of creation) no provision was made for an Incarnation of the Word. If the first human being had not sinned, the Incarnation would not have taken place. The Incarnation was "decreed" only after man had sinned, and so it derived entirely from that circumstance. To restore the primal world order—blighted by sin—the Son of God was born into this world as a man in order to set the human race once more upon the path to its ultimate destiny. In this account of things the link between Christ and the world is merely accidental. No Fall, no Incarnation. The cosmos had been created by God without any connection with the God-man. Through Christ's appearing on earth, however, the world, via man, has been hallowed and redeemed. From that moment a moral and juridical bond between Christ and the world comes into being : by virtue of his hypostatic union with the Word and of his merit as Redeemer he acquires a title to kingship over the entire world.

The distinguishing mark of this interpretation is of course the fact that it kept the divine decree regarding the Incarnation outside the original plan of creation and therefore accorded the Incarnation itself no place in the concrete order of things. This makes it difficult to say specifically what place Christ has in the world. It is only within a sinful humanity that he has any function to fulfil : the function of Redeemer, from which a state of moral and juridical relatedness to the whole world ensues as a consequence. There could be no question, in that case, of a function, conceived in organic terms, within the whole of the cosmic order.

Very different from this is the Scotist interpretation, as it is called. In this view, which appeals to numerous texts in the Scriptures and numbers among its advocates such great names as those of St. Francis de Sales, Newman and Scheeben, Christ is held to be the goal and crowning-point not only of the supernatural but of the natural order. Right from the beginning—that is to say, quite independently of the Fall—the whole creation was planned with the God-man in view. Even if man had not sinned, the Word would have become man; for the truth

is that Christ is the supreme revelation of God in this world
and the masterpiece of God's creation. It seems hard to
believe that this disclosure would only have taken place on the
assumption that man would first have committed sin. The
Incarnation was contained, therefore, in the original plan of
creation. The Fall introduced only an accidental change in
this : the God-man, who had been conceived as the goal and
crown of the whole created order, would also through his
sufferings and death act as the redeemer of all mankind.

Thus this interpretation ascribes to Christ a central function
in the cosmos—a function, that is, not to be understood in
purely moral or juridical terms. In its very existence the world
is centred on Christ—and not *vice versa*, as the first interpretation avers. In the beginning it was orientated upon him, so
that we are indeed right to say that he is the beginning and
the end, the Alpha and Omega, of all things. Christ's place in
the cosmos is an organic function : that is, the world is centred
on Christ in respect of its intrinsic structure, in its actual mode
of being, so that—to use St. Paul's expression—he " is in all
things pre-eminent ".[35] In this context also E. Schillebeeck
writes : " We may, and indeed we must, say that the One who
is risen from the dead is the purport and centre of the concrete creation, even insofar as it was *not as yet* sinful : namely,
in Adam."[36]

This is not the place to go more fully into the matter of
these two interpretations. They both have their right to exist
in Catholic theology; and both are entirely consonant with the
fundamental tenets of Christianity. This is a case of an " open
question ", concerning which every Christian may think whatever appears to him to accord best with the evidence of Scripture and the tradition of the Church. If we have recalled these
interpretations offered by traditional theology here, it is in
order to demonstrate that the question of Christ's place in the
created order is in no sense a new question which Teilhard has
thrown up, and at the same time to show that what we have
here is an issue allowing of further development.

The place accorded to this problem in most manuals of

theology is only a secondary one. Often it is just treated as a
kind of historical reminiscence to which only a more or less
academic interest attaches—although in earlier centuries it did,
of course, exert a certain influence on the spiritual temper of
the two schools. In Teilhard's view, however, what is at issue
here is a very relevant and very present problem; and finding
the answer to it, as he believed, may well help us in no small
measure to build up a spirituality attuned to the spiritual and
intellectual needs of contemporary man. That is why he
centred his attention on this problem in theology. The principal task of theology to-day consists, as he believed, in this :
" to analyse the relationship, in the matter of existence and
influence which links together Christ and the Universe "[37]; " to
elucidate the very Catholic idea of Christ Alpha and
Omega ".[38] " The truth is, the keystone of the arch which has
to be erected lies in our hands. If we want to achieve the so
much needed synthesis between faith in God and faith in the
world, then the best possible thing for us to do is to bring to
the fore on a dogmatic basis, in the person of Christ, the cosmic
aspect and the cosmic function which make him organically the
principle and controlling force, the very *soul* of evolution."[39]

ii *The Place of Christ in the Cosmos*

The view that Teilhard developed regarding the place which
accrues to Christ in the whole of cosmic history shows a great
affinity with the so-called Scotist interpretation.[40] For Teilhard too the entire creation centres upon Christ as its natural
crowning-point, so that the order of creation is inconceivable
without him. One is struck by the fact that the scriptural
passages which Teilhard adduces in support of his opinion are
the very same ones as are cited by the champions of the
Scotist interpretation. Yet there are also important points of
difference to be stressed, which spring from a different conception of the structure of the universe. The cosmos that Teilhard envisages is obviously quite different from the picture of

the world which forms the background to mediaeval theology. The whole point of the exercise, for him, is to indicate the place of Christ in a creation with an evolving and convergent character. He believes that this new world view offers a better chance of understanding Christ's place and function than was the case with the earlier one.

As he saw it, there was not really much chance of being able to indicate the place that Christ occupied in the world, so long as it was statically conceived; for such a view was bound to remain tied to purely extrinsic and juridical concepts. Men attributed a "kingship" (what an antiquated sound that metaphor has!) to Christ, a "kingship" over the created order, a "kingship" conferred upon him by the Father, and one to which he was "morally entitled" by virtue of his redeeming death. Thenceforward everything was subject, therefore, to his juridical authority. *Rex regum et dominus dominantium.* Any question of an organic link between Christ and the world simply does not come into it—and indeed could hardly do so. In a world mechanistically and statically conceived there just was no really central place which one could point to as adequately representing the dignity and status of Christ.

But in the perspective of the new view of the world the situation is quite altered. Here one can indeed indicate a point which governs the whole of cosmic evolution, forms the keystone and climax of it and exerts a power of attraction giving to the whole evolutive process its intrinsic drive and orientation. This universal cosmic centre of human—and thus also of cosmic—evolution, in which everything is bound in the end to attain its unity and consummation, is signalized in the phenomenology of the universe by the term: the Omega point.

Is not this precisely the place which according to Christian doctrine is to be ascribed to Christ? Do not the characteristics of the point Omega meet all the requirements that we must lay down in this case. Is not our whole insight into the mystery of Christ hereby deepened in a fruitful and wonderful way, wholly consonant with St. Paul's teaching? "If we

pursue the perspectives of science as they relate to the humanization process to their logical and final conclusion, we then
discover the climax of anthropogenesis to be the existence of
an ultimate centre or focus of personality and consciousness
which is indispensable for the orientation of the historical
growth of spirit and for its synthesis. Now this *Omega point*
(as I have called it), is it not the ideal centre from which
to see radiating the Christ whom we worship—a Christ whose
supernatural lordship is accompanied, as we are aware, by a
predominating physical power over the natural spheres of the
world? *In quo omnia constant.* Marvellous coincidence, indeed,
of the data of faith with the processes of reason itself! What at
first appeared to be a threat instead turns out to be a splendid
confirmation. Far from coming into opposition with Christian
dogma, the vastly increased importance assumed by man in
nature results (when considered exhaustively) in traditional
Christology being given a new lease of relevance and a new
vitality."[41]

For Teilhard there can be no real doubt. " Christ occupies
for us, *hic et nunc*, so far as his position and *function* are
concerned, the place of the point Omega."[42] To persuade
ourselves of this we have only to look at the most traditional
data supplied by Christianity and the most authentic utterances
of Holy Writ regarding the status and function of Christ.
Everything has its being in him. Everything is brought into
unity by him. In him everything finds its completion, not only
in the order of grace but in that of nature too.[43] In the
Christian idea of things the whole of history is directed
toward the building up and unifying of the entire human
race into a supranatural community of which Christ is the
head and all of us the members. Christianity has an essentially
eschatological character. It bids us look toward the future,
toward the realization of the Kingdom of God. Christianity's
vision of the future is a vision of a supernatural and definitive
unity, a unity built up and held together by a personal centre,
the historic Christ, whose return at the end of the Age we now
await. The doctrine of the Mystical Body, which St. Paul

and St. John expressed under a variety of images and similes, is one of the most central data of the Christian tradition. " The essence of Christianity is nothing more or less than a belief in the world's coming to be one in God through the Incarnation."[44]

Thus when one sets the perspectives of science alongside those of faith, one simply cannot escape the impression that both are converging toward one and the same point. How could it be otherwise? If that were not the case, then we would have to conclude that Christ is no longer in the full sense of the word the world's crowning point and consummation, since there would be, beyond him, yet another climax and consummation. " It is in fact to Christ that we direct our gaze when, to whatever degree of approximation it may be, we look forward to some higher Pole of humanization and personalization."[45] For Teilhard then, Christ is the goal and crown of the natural as of the supernatural order—a position wholly compatible with the strictest orthodoxy. Of course, there is an important distinction to be made between the two perspectives. The one relates to the plane of nature, the other to that of the supernature. The one operates in the plane of creation, the other in the plane of grace. But let us not lose sight of the fact that whilst there is indeed a distinction between nature and grace, there is no separation; that they interpenetrate each other and that the distinction which we draw between various " planes " in the work of God conceals a large measure of anthropomorphism. God's work is *one* work. As the classic formula puts it, grace does not annul nature but on the contrary assumes, ennobles and exalts it. Ought we not to say, therefore, that the supernatural unification of mankind presupposes a natural unification and indeed elevates it to a supreme dignity and completion (in a higher order)? One of the things that theology has always said, surely, is that nature is ordered upon supernature, so that it is perfectly legitimate to exhibit the harmony existing between them.

It has sometimes been argued that this way of representing Christ does not have much to do with the historic Christ of the gospel. But arguments of this sort rest on a false assumption. "Against this elevation of the historic Christ to a universal physical function, against this ultimate identification of cosmogenesis with Christogenesis, it has sometimes been objected that such a conception involves the risk of causing the human reality of Jesus to fade away into the super-human or to vanish into the cosmic. Nothing would seem to me more ill founded than this misgiving. The more, in fact, one considers the fundamental laws of evolution, the more one becomes convinced that the universal Christ would not be able to appear at the end of time, unless he had previously inserted himself into the course of the world's movement *by way of birth*, in the form of an *element*. If it is really by Christ-Omega that the universe is held in movement, on the other hand, it is from his concrete source, the Man of Nazareth, that Christ-Omega (theoretically and historically) derives for our experience his whole stability."[46] In other words : without a historic Christ there could be no mystical body of Christ, no total Christ.

Certain of Teilhard's expressions and turns of phrase may on occasion strike one who is used to the traditional formulas of theology as, to begin with, rather disconcerting. If, however, we transpose his ideas into a more traditional language, it soon becomes apparent that the basic idea that he is trying to get across ties in to a large extent with one of the most ancient schools of thought in Catholic theology—always granting, of course, that he combines this theological interpretation of his with a world view which was utterly unknown to earlier centuries but now imparts a new background, a new dimension, to the traditional figure of Christ. We may sum up Teilhard's understanding of the matter in the words of Claude Cuénot : " On the one hand you have the Christ of Christian mysticism . . . described with such deep feeling by Paul. On the other you have the cosmic pole which is a postulate of modern science and is necessary in the whole new picture that we have of the world, in order to draw together at its apex, and so to unify, ascending evolution. Now Teilhard was of the opinion that between these two poles there must exist a degree of correspondence, of homogeneity and, at bottom, an ultimate identity. Only at a later stage will the fact of this coincidence, of this identity, permeate into the consciousness of men; and only at the end of time will it find its consummation in the Parousia. Then science and mysticism will fuse together. Then the two poles will reach a condition of mutual influence, so that an interchange of attributes can ensue, and Christ envelops the entire cosmos, whilst the Christified cosmos itself becomes an object of love."[47]

ii *Christ as the Meaning of History*

Teilhard believed, therefore, that the place which we must assign to Christ in the universe coincides with the place denoted in his scheme of the world by the point Omega. But what does such an identification really mean? What does such a thesis imply?

It implies, of course, in the first place what we said earlier on : that Christ is linked, not simply in a moral or juridical context but as it were structurally and organically with the cosmos. In and with the very process of creation the world is orientated upon him. All things are created in him : *in ipso condita sunt universa.*[48]

Secondly, it implies that through Christ the world acquires its ultimate unity and cohesion. The point Omega is indeed the element that imparts to the whole of cosmic evolution its final unity—the point at which multiplicity is reduced to unity and on which all the threads of history converge. It is just such a function that we are to ascribe to Christ. He is the cornerstone in God's plan for the world. In him, as St. Paul says, all things are brought to unity : *Omnia in ipso constant.*[49]

It implies in the third instance that Christ is the very meaning of history. The point Omega gives to evolution its orientation : *de facto*, evolution is focussed upon this final term;

and at the deepest level its laws are governed and regulated by this final goal. Even this property of the point Omega can be assigned to Christ. In the Christian perspective he is truly the meaning of history, in that everything is centred on him. The whole world order is to be discovered in St. Paul's words : *omnia vestra sunt, vos autem Christi, Christus autem Dei.*[50] The entire lower world is centred in man—but man is centred in Christ, and Christ in God. Transposed into Teilhard's terms, this notion may be expressed as follows : cosmogenesis eventuates through biogenesis in a noogenesis; but the noogenesis is consummated in a Christogenesis. " The Universe," wrote Henri Bergson, " is a machine for making gods." As Teilhard envisaged it, we could say that the v orld is an instrument for realizing the total Christ. Looked at from this standpoint, Christ really does govern and control the vast abysses of time and space. However brief the span of his earthly life— now two thousand years ago—there is nothing to prevent his constituting the axis and the apex of a universal process of maturation.[51]

Lastly, this thesis implies that Christ is the great source of power and energy which is drawing all things toward itself. From him there radiates an influence which in the final instance nothing can escape. " Being so situated [in our world view] Christ must necessarily, whatever the ultimately supernatural character of his domain, exert his radiating influence by degrees over the whole body of nature. Since, in the concrete sense, there is but one synthesizing process taking place *from top to bottom* in the universe, it follows that no element whatsoever, no movement at any level of the world, can exist outside the *informing* influence of the main centre of things. Thus, already co-extensive with space and time, Christ, by reason of his position at the world's central point, is also automatically co-extensive with the scale of values which extend from the peaks of Spirit to the depths of matter."[52]

So we can see that the various attributes which Holy Scripture ascribes to Christ, far from being even partly undermined or lessened, within the context of the new world view acquire their most comprehensive and most concrete significance. So far as essentials are concerned, such an interpretation is in every respect at one with the views which the Greek Fathers developed regarding Christ's place in the universe, and which in Byzantine art found expression in the figure of Christ *Pantokrator*.

Teilhard recapitulated this doctrine in terms which at first sight seem strange to us. He talks about "the Universal Christ", about "Christ the Evolver", about "the Super-Christ", about "the Christic". We must not allow ourselves to be put off by these unfamiliar expressions. In point of fact what they are really saying, when put back into the framework of the modern view of the world, is part and parcel of the Christian tradition and of its most authentic content. If Teilhard had had to limit his activities to the theological field, then he would perhaps have stated these things in more traditional terms and concepts. But as he was a man of science and was addressing himself to the men of today who live within these new perspectives, that circumstance was bound to affect his language and mode of expression.

The doctrine that even in the order of nature Christ is the goal and head of the whole creation is one of extraordinary richness; and we shall see in more detail to what important conclusions it can lead us. That a deeper theological treatment of it is much to be desired can scarcely be denied, therefore. Meanwhile, Teilhard is unquestionably right when he argues that his conception of Christ fits perfectly with that of Holy Scripture. In particular he is right in saying that Christians generally do not attach sufficient importance to a doctrine which is nevertheless fundamental to Christianity : namely, that of Christ's return at the end of the Age. "On the horizon of the Christian world the Parousia (that is, the return of Christ in glory at the end of time) occupies a central place— something which, because men have awaited it over so many centuries, is easily forgotten. In this unique and supreme event, in which (as the Faith instructs us) the historic is to be fused with the Transcendental, the mystery of the Incarnation

culminates and is manifested with the realism of a physical
' elucidation' of the universe."[53]

In a Christian perspective it is conceivable, therefore, that
this moment of Christ's Parousia should coincide with the
moment at which mankind will have attained its natural
completion: namely, in the moment Omega. In a sense, this
natural completion would form the condition, as it were, for
the second coming of Christ at the end of the Age. " Christ's
first coming to earth was only feasible—and nobody will dispute this—after the human species, in the setting of the general
process of evolution, had been anatomically constituted and
from the social standpoint had attained in some degree a
collective consciousness. If this much be granted, why not go a
step further and ask whether in the case of his second and
last coming *also*, Christ defers his return until the human
community has realized to the full its *natural* potentialities,
and thereby becomes qualified to receive through him its supernatural consummation? Indeed, if the historical development
of spirit is bound by definite physical rules, must not this be
equally the case—*a fortiori*, even—where its further unfolding
and completion are concerned?"[54]

Theologically speaking, such a line of argument is surely
acceptable. Furthermore, the quotation is of special interest
because it illustrates so very well that contrary to what some
critics have averred Teilhard distinguishes very clearly between
the natural and the supernatural order and plainly declares
that the natural completion of mankind can at most constitute a
condition, and *not* a cause, of its supernatural consummation.
The second coming of Christ, like the first, has the character
of a free and unmerited gift.

Thus we are to understand the whole of history as an ascent
of the whole world toward its consummation in the natural
and supernatural order—and the two forms of completion do
not in any way conflict. " And when all things have been subjected to him, then shall the Son also himself be subjected to
the One who subjected all things to him, that God may be all
in all."[55]

iv *The Problem of Evil*

It should be evident from what we have just been saying with what great sympathy Teilhard approached the problem of the place occupied by Christ in cosmic evolution as a whole. The entire world is orientated on Christ, not through Redemption only but through Creation as well; and even within the natural order its completion is to be found in him—in whom, as St. Paul says, everything consists. The point Omega of science must therefore, as he believed, ultimately coincide in the Christian consciousness with the Christ of faith. The whole world as historical event is for him " a vast phenomenon of Christification."[56] Having first been manifested as a biogenesis and a noogenesis, the cosmic eventualizing process culminates finally in Christogenesis.[57] For him the whole of evolution is in the last instance an ascent to Christ. All that has value, all that we meet with in the world that is true and good, points us to him.

But goodness and truth are not all that we encounter in the world. There are also evil and the lie; and in the Christian perspective there is sin—and original sin into the bargain. Inevitably, then, we are brought face to face with a further problem : the problem of physical and moral evil. Here we come to one of the most delicate and most controversial points in Teilhard's thesis.[58]

Let us confine ourselves to the purely phenomenal aspect of evil, leaving aside any approach to the metaphysical problem, which was in any case handled by Teilhard only in a fragmentary way. What place does evil have in the concrete order of things? We live in a universe in evolution : that is to say, in a world that is not only subject to continuous change but ought to be envisaged rather as a process of growth toward ever higher states of complexity. Step by step the world is being built up : in other words, the world is growing out of relatively imperfect states into more perfect ones. In a world of that sort evil is inevitable. Whatever has yet to be completed is of necessity imperfect, defective, unfinished. Evil is thus *structurally* part and parcel of a world in evolution. An evolving world and a perfect world—these are mutually contradictory ideas. Evolution is a laborious and tentative process of questing, of trying things out; so that disaster, pain, suffering and death are its inevitable concomitants. In a world of this sort evil is no fortuitous occurrence, no accidental phenomenon. On the contrary it is an essential aspect of an evolutionary process which has to pick its way through a maze of errors and miscarriages of effort. Since God willed to create a world that must grow to its completion via an evolutive process, imperfection and evil were bound to occur in this creation. It could not be otherwise.

Just as it is impossible for God to make a square circle, for instance—because such a thing is inherently contradictory and therefore absurd—so it is impossible for him to create a world that would be at once perfect and yet bound to attain its perfection by the road of evolution. An evolving world and a perfect world are as intrinsically contradictory as a square circle and so are fundamentally impossible in conjunction.

But besides physical evil there is also moral evil—sin. As soon as evolution has reached the stage at which man appears —as a being possessed of reflective consciousness and freedom —moral evil enters the world. For man too is an imperfect and incomplete being. So long as he has not reached the end to which he is destined, sin remains possible. The higher his consciousness and freedom rise, the more his power to do both good and evil increases. As Teilhard saw it, therefore, sin is statistically inevitable in evolutive mankind. From a phenomenological viewpoint evil is a by-product of evolution. " Disharmony or physical disintegration among the pre-living, suffering among the living, sin in the sphere of freedom; there is no *order under formation* which does not at every stage involve disorder."[59]

Evil, then, is a universal phenomenon in a world in evolution; and it assumes different forms in the various categories of

things and beings which turn up in the course of evolution.
So long as ultimate order has not been realized, disorder is in
fact inherent in the structure of things, as a permanent possibility. It has sometimes been alleged that Teilhard paid no
attention to the problem of evil, and that in consequence his
view of the world was marked by an excessive optimism.
Without any doubt this sort of allegation rests on a mistake.
Teilhard certainly did recognize the existence of evil—nay,
more, in his view of things evil acquires a cosmic dimension, in that it constitutes a phenomenon attendant upon the
whole of evolution and one that is indeed statistically inevitable in a world whose completion can only be realized
through a protracted and difficult struggle. If he was optim-
istic, it was not because he underestimated the place of evil in
the world, but because he was convinced that in the end good
will triumph over evil, order over chaos.

It is precisely because evil has such a large place in the
world that the latter stood in such radical need of redemption. For the very reason that evil has this cosmic dimension
the redemption by Christ must have a truly cosmic dimension
as well. His cross comes to have a new and all-embracing
significance here. "Projected onto the background of such a
universe (that is, of a universe in evolution) with which the
battle with evil forms the *conditio sine qua non* of existence,
the cross assumes a new gravity and a fresh beauty—the very
qualities calculated to appeal to and captivate us the most.
Of course, Jesus remains the one who bears the sins of the
world: moral evil is in some mysterious way compensated
for by suffering. But more essentially, even, is he the one who
in himself and in behalf of us all structurally overcomes the
resistance to the ascendancy of spirit, which is inherent in
matter. He it is who bears the weight—inevitable by virtue of
its construction—of every kind of creation. He is the symbol
and gesture of progress. The total and definitive meaning of
redemption lies not only in expiation but in breakthrough
and conquest."[60]

Catholic theology has always distinguished two aspects in

the redemptive work of Christ : a negative aspect—the expiation and taking away of sin—and a positive aspect—the exaltation and sanctification of man. Teilhard preserves both these aspects in full; but within his vision of the world they acquire a broader significance. The evil that is to be overcome is principally moral evil, as that is committed by man; but it embraces all deficiencies, so to speak, which are present in the cosmos by virtue of its evolutive character. First and foremost, man's supernatural enrichment and exaltation must be the fruit of grace; but in the natural order too man and the world (with precisely their supernatural sanctification in view) have to be brought to their ultimate destiny. There is nothing to forbid our thinking that this ascent in the natural plane is also affected by Christ.

Of course, it can never be emphasized enough that man's salvation can only be brought about, in the end, by grace. But —and on this point Teilhard opens up to us new vistas which it is for theology to explore at a deeper level[61]—the natural order can also be of service to the supernatural and is actually indispensable to it. Even in this order of nature—in keeping with the Scotist interpretation which we cited earlier on and with which Teilhard, perhaps unconsciously, accords so well— we may be permitted to recognize the saving and redeeming effect of Christ, so that he can be called, in the full sense of the term, the *Saviour of the World.* Thus the cross is not only the symbol of atonement for sin, but also " the dynamic and comprehensive symbol of a world whose condition is one of personalizing evolution "[62]—an evolution that can in turn contribute (albeit only indirectly) to the building up of the Mystical Body.

All this makes it quite clear that in all his thoughts and observations on the Incarnation and Redemption Teilhard was actuated by one major concern : to ascribe to Christ an all-embracing position in the totality of a world whose evolutive and convergent character he had discerned—a position that made Christ the centre of the whole world-event in the natural as in the supernatural order. One of the biggest

dangers for Christianity, as he believed, was the very fact that
so many Christians were still tying their notion of Christ to a
mediaeval cosmology, instead of setting it firmly and deliberately within the new temporal and spatial dimensions with
which science presents us and in which the gospel message—
and especially Paul's teaching about Incarnation and Redemption—actually acquire a much greater and more profound significance.

v *Growth toward Unity*

Teilhard confessed that his mind was ruled by an irresistible
hankering after organic unity and cohesion. The kind of all-
embracing synthesis to which this urge led him is by now
more or less evident. When on a basis of his researches and
insights as a scientist he had projected a coherent picture of
the universe—a universe that presented itself to him as a great
spatio-temporal whole with a dynamic and convergent structure—he applied himself to the task of constructing a synthesis
on a higher plane between this world view and Christianity.

In making this attempt he took as his starting-point—in
contrast to Lecomte du Nouÿ, who confined his terms of
reference almost exclusively to Christian ethics—the most
central and fundamental doctrine of Christianity : the doctrine
of the Incarnation and the Redemption. What does it mean
that God has become man in an evolving world and that God
has redeemed that world? This was the question that he tried
to answer—and to answer in closest possible conformity with
the traditional insights of Catholic theology, only setting them
within the framework of the new view of the world.

Out of this twofold reflection and rumination on the world
and on Christianity there grew of its own accord, as it were,
the synthesis which he was aiming at. All things find their
unity in the person of Christ, who is their beginning and
their end. The whole history of the world may be summed up
in the terms : cosmogenesis, biogenesis, noogenesis, Christo-

genesis. The orders of creation and of redemption, of nature and of grace, however distinct from each other they may be, ultimately constitute an unsurpassable unity. We are now in a position to understand the passage which we quoted earlier on : " The major event of my life has been the gradual identification on the horizon of my soul of two sources of illumination, the first being the point of cosmic culmination postulated by a universal process of evolution, of a convergent type, and the other formed by the risen Christ of the Christian faith."[63]

Thus Christianity was for him the religion of evolution in the full sense of the term. " Catholicism had at first view disappointed me by its narrow, constricted way of presenting the world and its failure to grasp the significant role of matter. I see now, however—following the incarnate God whom Christianity discloses to me—that I can only be saved as an integral part of the universe. . . . The total Christ is only consummated and is only attainable at the end of universal evolution. In him I have found what my very being dreamt of : a personalized universe by whose domination I am personalized. And this *soul of the world* rises up before me not simply as the fragile creation of my individual thinking, but as the product of a long, historical revelation in which even the most sceptical are surely bound to recognize one of the principal forces directing human progress."[64]

Christ, then, was the point of impact at which the two poles of his thinking—God and the universe—met together, and his inner dialectical state was resolved in a higher synthesis. The whole cosmic event and the whole of human history at once became a reality charged with meaning. The world is not absurd; history is not blind chance : they have a meaning, a direction and a goal. Through every vicissitude and revolution, through all the ups and downs, through moments of advance and of temporary relapse, the mighty course of the world's history takes its way and draws on toward its definitive and inavertible goal : the disclosure of the total Christ, crowned and adorned with the riches of the entire cosmos, at the end of the Age : " This unique and supreme event in which the historic is to be fused with the transcendental."[65] That is why Christ is for every Christian, in the fullest sense of the word, the meaning and the goal of history.

In the light of this theology of history the question may well be asked to what extent a right line of approach to history also means a right attitude regarding the Kingdom of God. O. A. Rabut writes about this : " To be ' right with history,' so to speak, is not necessarily to be ' right with God '."[66] It would seem to us that this is a rather ambiguous proposition. Admittedly, the natural perfecting of man and his supernatural salvation are two different things. The spiritual perfection of mankind is not an automatic consequence of evolution or of history. In the final instance man's true salvation can only be the effect of grace. Yet this does not mean that up to a certain point (i.e. as a necessary, but by itself insufficient, condition) man's perfection in the natural plane is not requisite for his supranatural completion—or to put it another way : that his natural perfection cannot be made to subserve his supernatural destiny. If Christ is in the full sense the meaning of history, does it not follow that a right line with regard to history must also carry with it, in some measure, a correct approach to the Kingdom of God? Must not anyone whose position vis-à-vis the Kingdom of God is wrong necessarily have a wrong attitude also regarding history; so that every attitude which deliberately repudiates that goal amounts to a betrayal of the real meaning of history too? For the Christian a right approach to history is only conceivable if at the same time and in the first place it involves a right attitude to the Kingdom of God.

If Christ, then, is the meaning of history, it at once becomes possible to understand what place the Church must have in the history of mankind. From the Christian viewpoint the Church cannot possibly be a marginal phenomenon or a fortuitous by-product, since she is the instrument, as it were, by means of which Christ's completion, his " pleromatization ", is brought about. On an external view she presents herself to us as a " phylum ",[67] which with its roots in the past grows and develops through all the political, social and cultural vicissitudes of history. In her deepest being, however, she is a centre of divine power, gathering together the scattered race of men and carrying it upward to its ultimate unity in Christ : " At the very heart of the social phenomenon a kind of *ultra-socialization* is in progress, by means of which the *Church* is slowly taking shape, by bringing together through her influence all the spiritual energies of the noosphere in their most noble form and giving them life :—the Church that Christified part of the world aware of itself as such—the Church, principal focus of inter-human relationships through the intensity of its charity, the Church, central axis of universal convergence and the very spot where the universe and the Omega point come rushing together."[68]

When we learn to see Christ as the goal of the natural as well as the supernatural order, then from the Christian viewpoint the whole world takes on a meaningful and organic unity : " For anyone who has once grasped the nature of a world in which cosmogenesis, focussed and centred upon anthropogenesis, culminates in Christogenesis—for such an individual everything, every element and every contingency in the universe, becomes illumined, aglow, animated and infinitely lovable."[69]

Chapter 6

TOWARDS A NEW CHRISTIAN
HUMANISM

Teilhard had asked himself " how . . . we can reconcile, and provide mutual nourishment for, the love of God and the healthy love of the world, a striving towards detachment and a striving towards the enrichment of our human lives ".[70] We can now see a solution to this problem beginning to take shape. Once the Christian perspective had been conjoined with that of natural science, there emerged automatically, as it were, a field of action in which human activity could be fully deployed and could expand to its maximal capacity.

In the centuries now lying behind us it had often seemed as though the efforts and aspirations of men were being pulled in two different directions. The call of earth and the call of God appeared to be mutually exclusive factors.

It is true that within the Christian consciousness there was, strictly speaking, no clash between these two duties. The very first words that God addressed to man in the Bible had actually invited him to apply himself wholeheartedly to his earthly task and its fulfilment : " Populate the earth, and subdue it."[71] Even so, in the concrete circumstances of the Christian's life there persisted a certain tension between the mundane, profane matters which made up the greater part of his daily routine and those rare and lofty moments in which the individual could really turn in love and adoration toward God. The masters of the spiritual life taught us that we could to some extent relieve this tension by carrying out our profane tasks for love of God and in obedience to his will, using them as a means of self-denial and hallowing them by understanding them aright. All this was perfectly fair. And yet it still was not clear how our work could be *intrinsically* sanctified. The intention was still to impart to it a wholly external quality of consecration. Every endeavour to progress in knowledge and to enhance " the beauty of the earth ", to achieve social justice or to add to and enrich the life of man on earth, was still relegated to the sphere of the profane—and " profane " was a term commonly charged with a certain pejorative significance.

But for anyone who recognizes in Christ the final goal and crown, not only of the supernatural order but of the natural order too (a thesis that is completely defensible from a theological standpoint), or who, like Teilhard, gives this view an even more concrete expression by ascribing to Christ the place denoted in our world scheme by the Omega point, this tension is resolved once and for all. Such a recognition makes it possible—far more than was previously the case—for him to give his full attention to mundane tasks and problems and to expend himself upon them in the conviction that ultimately they have an *intrinsic* orientation toward Christ and God and so possess an intrinsic value and consecration within the total Christian world order.

Regarded in this light, the life of the Christian acquires a majestic and impressive unity, in which earthly preoccupations and concerns find their proper place along with his supernatural aspirations—and full justice is done to the intrinsic connection between the two. Since the true and final end of history consists in the consummation of the integral Christ, and since an indispensable (albeit insufficient) condition of that is the building up of the human community in a higher collective consciousness, it follows that all activity on man's part which in some measure contributes to mankind's ascent toward this goal is also, in the last analysis, calculated to further the coming of that Kingdom to which the Scriptures bid us look forward so eagerly. Aspiring to union with God --and believing in our final destiny—no longer distracts us from our earthly task or alienates us from the work that is ours to accomplish in this world. Quite the reverse; for the love of Christ becomes the great source of inspiration for our activity even in the temporal plane, because we know that this work of ours is needed and is intrinsically orientated on Christ. " Hence whatever our role as men may be, whether we are artists, working-men or scholars, we can, if we are Christians, speed towards the object of our work as though towards an opening on to the supreme fulfilment of our beings."[72] So far, then, from seducing our attention from our task here on earth or promoting an attitude of indifference to the toils and activities of men, Christianity offers us an unparalleled and certainly unsurpassed incentive to fulfil our earthly duties and to fulfil them well, just as it affords to all human labour its finest quality of consecration. From this whole line of thought can be derived a profound and comprehensive theology of human work.

Teilhard was conscious that all this is in complete conformity with the Church's doctrine. " What I am doing is . . . simply to substitute for the juridical terms in which the Church has couched her faith terms borrowed from physical reality ".[73] It has sometimes been argued that in this way of presenting things the distinction between the natural and supernatural orders is not sufficiently taken into account—as though the supernatural uniting of all Christians in the Mystical Body were a consequence of mankind's completion in a higher unity at the natural level. Such an idea is completely out of keeping, however, with Teilhard's most explicit declarations about this. " I do not attribute any definitive or absolute value to the varied constructions of nature. What I like about them is not their particular form, but their function, which is to build up mysteriously, first what can be divinised, and then, through the grace of Christ coming down upon our endeavour, what is divine. . . ."[74] So far as he is concerned, the natural completion of the human race has an indispensable but still only preparatory role to fulfil. " That there should be an apex to the cosmos is just as necessary to Christ's consummation as was the presence of a woman to his conception."[75] The gratuitous character of salvation, as also of the Incarnation, is fully preserved in this view of things.

In this perspective, therefore, the life of the Christian, in both its earthly and its heavenly dimension, takes on a profound and organic unity. In this perspective it becomes possible to be centred wholly upon God and at the same time to throw all one's resources into the struggle for progress in this world. In this perspective too we may love the earth dearly without any disloyalty to our heavenly calling. "At one time the impression was abroad that only two possibilities were logically open to man : to love either heaven or earth. In the new mental dimension we are able to see a third way : to journey heavenwards by the earthly road. Through the world there is an (authentic) communion with God."[76] "Without lapsing into any kind of naturalism or Pelagianism, the believer discovers that as much as—nay, even more than—any unbeliever, he can and must apply himself eagerly to the earth's advancement, as a condition of the consummation of the Kingdom of God."[77]

Far from alienating man from himself—as Marxism alleges —religion, when interpreted in this way, becomes the supreme source of spiritual energy, from which we can draw the strength to accomplish our task here on earth as perfectly as may be. "The Christian alone (and this *to the extent* to which he is imbued with the humano-divine attributes of the Universal Christ) is in a position today to respond to the many-voiced invitations of nature and grace by a *completely synthetised act* in which the spirit of tradition and the spirit of adventurous enquiry, the spirit of the earth and the spirit of God meet, supplement and stimulate each other."[78]

More and better than anyone else, therefore, the Christian is fitted to tackle with confidence and enthusiasm the great task which we have to fulfil in this world. He more than anyone else is able to listen—and to listen lovingly—to the call of the earth, arousing us and summoning us to complete the work already begun there. For him the threat of the *taedium vitae,* of despondency and despair, is overcome for good. Faith in Christ, so far from imposing any weakness or any restrictions on our will to exert ourselves, is the greatest incentive we can have to work confidently and to build the future. The stronger his love for God and Christ, the more the Christian will be able to consecrate and surrender himself to the effort needed in order to realize our earthly hopes and expectations, in the conviction that in so doing he is helping at the same time to bring the Kingdom of God nearer in this world. For him exertion and toil have come to be a communing with God through the world. "In a universe within which everything contributes to the gradual formation of spirit —which is uplifted by God into final union—every kind of work, in its palpable reality, becomes a path to sanctity and communion."[79]

i *The New Ethos*

From what we have been saying it is clear how much Christianity can hallow and consecrate human toil. This applies not only to what we undertake as individuals. Of course, even the simplest and humblest work which we have to perform day by day is a necessary and valuable contribution to the upward progress of mankind. There is the labour of the working man, the business of the engineer and the factory manager, the toil of the housewife, nurse and social worker, of the teacher, doctor and civil servant. All this, in the last instance, is in the service of the spirit and of the future. These and so many other avocations find their meaning within the greater whole and have an intrinsic bearing on the Kingdom of God, in that they are a preparation for it.

But then these individual tasks and duties are not the whole story. There are also the great collective enterprises with which mankind is aware of being confronted today. It looks as though contemporary man has been seized with an unprecedented passion for creative activity in every field, as though he has suddenly become conscious not only of his power and potentialities but even more of his responsibility toward the future and toward the cosmos. A new horizon of tasks and challenges has suddenly been opened up before him. A mighty hope, a great expectancy, a passion for work never known before have mastered us and now actuate the most dynamic and highminded part of mankind.

In the scientific and social fields there are now tens of thousands of the best and most highly gifted people among us, working and pursuing their researches with a keenness and dedication never dreamt of before; and this fervour, this enthusiasm, are inspired not so much by motives of self-preservation or personal advantage, but much more by a high moral concern, which moves us to give of our best and highest powers in the pursuit of more truth, beauty and justice among men. "Underlying the awareness that by adding to the stature of mankind we are adding also to the world's stature is a tremendous moral impetus which to an ever increasing extent is becoming the *normal and accustomed driving force* behind all human activity."[80] As human beings and as Christians, we can react to the great communal endeavour engaging mankind today only with feelings of astonishment, tempered with respect and awe. But beyond that, if we are truly aware of the claims which Christianity makes upon us, we shall try to play our full part in this endeavour and feel within ourselves, as deeply as anyone can, the strong urge to co-operate in the splendid tasks now being shouldered by our contemporaries. Indeed, as Christians we should be standing in the very forefront, giving a lead to the best and finest activities of modern men.

The opposition between "siding with man" and "siding with God", which Sartre talks about in his *Lucifer and the Good Lord*, is a forced contrast which for Teilhard was quite unthinkable. No one has felt more passionately than he did about the progress of mankind through science and social action; and what stimulated and sublimated that passionate feeling in him was precisely his love of Christ. Admittedly, that has not always been the case with Christian people—as he frankly admits : " Let us be honest about this : only gradually has the Church come to recognize and to value—as we now do—the noble pride of men and the passion for systematic enquiry—those twin fundamental pillars of modern thought."[81]

His finest message to his brothers in the faith was exactly this : that they should devote themselves and all their powers to their task here on earth and in that way strive after their supernatural salvation. We have to overcome, once for all, the mistakes of the past and show by our whole bearing just how much religion as an incentive can mean for the real progress of mankind. It is not enough to adopt a purely passive or waiting attitude. Christians ought to be the very last people to fall victim to " the demon of immobilism ".[82] They must do their part with enthusiasm and total commitment in working for advancement in every field.

Thus the approach to life that Teilhard urges upon us is pre-eminently an activist one; and—although at quite a different level and in another perspective—what he proclaims has an almost Nietzschean ring about it. " To attempt everything, and to persevere with it to the end, toward ever greater conscious-ness :—in a world whose spiritual transformation we have learned to recognize, that is the universal and supreme law of morality; to imprison power (save when it is a question of achieving yet more power)—that is sin."[83] He looks in the same direction for an enlargement of the Christian virtues. "*Love one another.* Does this essentially Christian attitude mean only that we are to alleviate the cares and sorrows of other men? Or does it not also imply that out of an active sympathy we should spend ourselves on behalf of the great body of mankind, not merely to heal its wounds but to parti-cipate in all its hopes and fears and in building it up in line with what creation demands?"[84] Christian love is something more than a drop of oil poured over the sufferings of our fellows. It is the great and all-embracing force that is to help us and thrust us on in our efforts to realize to the full what it is to be human, to be man. It is the authentic source of energy which man needs if he is going to bring his task to its final completion.

In the field of ethics Teilhard obviously applies the same method that he has followed in all other respects : the method, that is, of looking at everything within the larger framework of the whole. He is determined always to see man and every aspect of man's life in their cosmic dimensions, as related to and cohering with the large historical process in which we are involved as its conscious and active partners—nay more, as those who bear the responsibility for it.

Viewed in this way, ethics is more than just a series of prescriptions designed to regulate relationships between people. *First and foremost it is the process of our becoming conscious of our due place within the cosmos and of the task that we have to perform within the totality of things.* The Christian system of moral values is itself capable of being transposed onto the cosmic plane and can be completely in its element there without having to surrender anything of its distinctive and essential character. Not only so; for within the Christo-cosmic vision worked out by Teilhard it acquires a fresh lustre and beauty. " Worshipping used to mean : to prefer God above all things, by referring them all to him and sacrificing them to Him. Henceforward worshipping must mean dedicating oneself, body and soul, to God's work of creation and linking oneself with it in order to complete the world through our toil and exploration.

" Loving one's neighbour used to mean : to do him no harm and to heal his wounds. Henceforward Christian love—although never ceasing to be compassionate—must find its highest expression in our committing the whole of life to the cause of our common progress.

" To be pure used chiefly to mean : to abstain and to keep oneself unsullied. From now on, chastity must be understood primarily to involve sublimating the powerful impulses of the flesh and of every passion.

" Detachment used to mean : not concerning oneself with the things of earth and resorting to them as little as possible. Henceforward, the meaning of detachment must be to rise beyond and to aspire beyond every good and beautiful thing, one after another—and to do so precisely because of the love we bear them.

"Resignation used normally to mean : a passive acceptance of the universe as it is. From now on, resignation is to be permitted only to the wrestler,[85] fully spent in his struggle with the Angel.

"A new definition of sanctity—that is what we all, at this moment, stand more or less in need of ".[86]

ii *A Union of Thought and Life*

During the last months of his life Teilhard had it in mind to write an essay which was to have borne the title : " *Humanism and Humanism* ". The main idea that he wanted to develop in it is stated in a letter of 30th March 1955.[87] There were, he thought, two forms of humanism that ought to be clearly distinguished. First of all, there was the old humanism of the Greek type, which was primarily concerned to ensure man's fullest possible development in an aesthetic context (Plato, Renaissance). Over against this outmoded humanism, still dear to the hearts of so many of our contemporaries, a new humanism is now taking shape : " An evolutive neo-humanism, supported by the conviction of the existence of an *Ultra-Human*". The Greeks dreamed of the " harmoniously developed man ". We dream of a fully evolved man, of man rising beyond himself in order to reach his true goal in " the super-human ". " The humanism of the cosmos is outmoded and out-distanced and is making way for a humanism of cosmo-genesis. . . ."

Teilhard had no further opportunity to write that essay; but in a sense one might say that as it turned out his whole work was nothing if not a sustained attempt to comprehend this new humanism in all its aspects. With his exceptional knowledge of the natural sciences and with his receptiveness and sensitivity to the spiritual and intellectual trends of our time to assist him, he set out to give precise shape to the new ideal of humanity, already present and operative in most of us at an unconscious level. This new ideal, however much it may be rooted in a knowledge of the past, is totally orientated on the future and on the conquest of a higher stage of the great historical process in which we are implicated. " A new humanism is everywhere on the increase—through the irresistible play of co-reflection : no longer the humanism of equilibrium, but a humanism of movement, in which no value whatever—*and this is even, indeed especially, true in the field of religion*—is going to subsist, unless it leave room for, and be prepared to defer to, the claims of a cosmic, ultra-human future."[88]

Teilhard's originality consists in his having confronted this new humanism with the Christian interpretation of life. Although to the outside observer he must have appeared to be first and foremost a man of science who felt deeply about the advancement of his subject, nevertheless in his heart of hearts he was before everything a religious thinker, irresistibly attracted by the problems which this new humanism poses for Christianity. We have already seen the ways in which he tried to integrate the new humanism into Christianity. There is consequently a hard core of truth in which Paul Chauchard has written : " What is new in Teilhard is not the scientific facts nor yet his religious ideas, but the fact that the two worlds of science and of faith—which appear to most of our contemporaries as antagonistic or at least as being poles apart —in his case coincided in a marvellous union of thought and life."[89] In this striving after union, after a synthesis of religion and culture, he is again completely in line with Catholic tradition.

From ancient times up to the Renaissance the best Catholic thinkers and artists tried to achieve a harmonious union between the ideals of Greek culture and the perspectives provided by the Gospel. The greatest figures of the Patristic period, as well as the most prominent representatives of the Middle Ages of Christendom, were engaged in this endeavour, which reached a fresh climax in the age of humanism and the baroque. Despite outward differences there was a single view of man which remained fundamentally constant throughout all those centuries; just as man's conception of the universe continued pretty well unchanged during all that time, resting heavily, as it did, upon that of the ancient Greeks. Nowadays these ways of envisaging man and the world have suffered a profound change—although even now there is no shortage of people whose mental outlook still belongs to the world of yesterday.

Under the influence of the modern sciences our notion of man and the world has acquired a totally new look. The theory of evolution has routed the old doctrine of fixed species and has opened the way to a coherent and dynamic vision of the world and of man. The cosmos has assumed the character of a cosmogenesis, and man (anthropos) that of an anthropogenesis. That everything exhibits a historical dimension is a truth that has forced itself irresistibly upon us. And that has given birth to a new humanism which, being supported by this new insight, has made man fully conscious of his creative task and of his responsibility toward the world. Of a return to the old "humanism of equilibrium", which the Greeks held in such high esteem and which was for so many centuries the decisive standard for Western culture there can no longer be any question.

What the Christian thinker in our time is required to do is to confront the new humanism with the substance, the import, of the Christian message. In all strictness, this is a mandate very much harder to carry out than that which the thinkers of antiquity and of the later centuries had to fulfil. When they set about their work, the Christian message had not yet become part of the fabric of any one culture. The situation is quite different today. The gospel message has come down to us couched in the categories of Graeco-Roman thought and in the language-forms provided by the classical understanding of culture. Hence the Catholic thinker today has a more difficult task to fulfil than had his predecessors. First, he has to try and grasp the message of the Gospel in its pristine purity and to rid it of those adventitious forms in which by-gone centuries have clothed it. Such an undertaking presupposes a scrupulously careful study of the content of revelation, and some profound reflection upon it. Once this task of " getting back to the fountainhead " has been accomplished (and present-day theology and biblical studies have already provided some splendid results in this connection), then we can make the attempt to confront the imperishable core of the Christian revelation with the neo-humanism that is going to be the factor governing the minds of men in the centuries to come.

iii *The New Christian*

Such an enormous undertaking is not to be satisfactorily concluded by a single individual. Teilhard was well aware that a task of this magnitude can be accomplished only through the joint counsel and working together of all creative minds within the Church. All his efforts were directed primarily to making his fellow Christians realize what the problems are that confront modern man, and therefore the modern Christian. What he wanted was not so much to project a neat and definitive system as to work out a programme for further enquiry and to provide some of the materials which could help to build us a spiritual and intellectual home.

To put it concisely : his concern was to blaze a trail for the new type of Christian of his dreams—one in whom love for the task of living here on earth in an evolving world would coincide with a love for Christ, goal and crowning glory of that world; a Christian whose vision would be focussed upon the future and whose faith would take full account of the world's new dimensions; a Christian in whom openness toward all mundane values would be matched with an unconditional commitment to God. No one saw more clearly than Teilhard how dangerous it must be for Christianity to cling to an outmoded world view. He strove with all the power at his command to make us conscious of the danger, to give the Church a new buoyancy and a new lease of vital energy.

Yet his message was not for Christians only. It was addressed with equal emphasis to those who represent modern science and in particular to those who look to science as justifying an atheistic or non-religious approach to life. The main objection advanced by atheistic Marxism to the idea of God and to religion is this : that religion alienates man from himself and from his task here in this world. It does not repudiate transcendence altogether; but it restricts it to man, who must try through his creative activity and toil to " transcend " himself and raise himself to a higher degree of perfection. To go forward in his own strength—and in reliance upon that alone—is man's true role; and where that is concerned, religion always constitutes an estrangement, an alienation of man from himself and from his task.

Teilhard recognizes that this criticism was not always without foundation. There have indeed been forms of religiosity that have either diverted our attention entirely from our task on this earth or have commended a wholly passive attitude toward the things of this world. Such forms of religious pietism act as a brake on human progress. They no longer correspond with the religious feeling of our time, in that they fail to endorse the value of work and strenuous action in the temporal plane. Yet such criticism, however legitimate it may be in certain instances, does not touch the essential core of religion. In the context of Christianity as envisaged by Teilhard it actually makes no sense at all. So far from alienating man from himself or from his task on earth, belief in God can be the very strongest incentive to us to fulfil our earthly calling just as well as we possibly can. " God," wrote Jean Lacroix, " is not a ready-made solution to every problem but a reason to search for that solution, and withal a guarantee that it is not in the final instance absurd to look for meaning and purpose and to do creative things. Work is all the more a duty to the extent that it forms a bridge to a viewpoint which ceases to be that of the world."[90]

The person who has come to recognize that anthropogenesis has as its focal point a Christogenesis cannot help regarding this prospect as one which spurs him on to shoulder his task in this historical process and to make himself fully sensible of his responsibility.

But even that is not all. Religion may also act as an incentive to man to give all that he is and all that he has to the task of completing, of "consummating", the world. It is a question, however, whether without religion he would ever be equipped to do this. In what might be called a phenomenology of human behaviour Teilhard has pointed out the need—indeed the necessity—for a personal centre, if ever mankind is to aspire actively to unity. It is only through faith in an authentic transcendence that man can find the strength to overcome the snags and obstacles besetting him and threatening the success of his enterprises here on earth. Left to fend for himself, he is surely exposed to the risk of falling into despondency and despair, to the menace of *taedium vitae*, to the temptations of egoism and of enervating self-indulgence. Is it not a curious thing that the very countries where material welfare is most advanced are also those where people most frequently resort to the use of all sorts of narotics and where the incidence of suicide is highest. Atheism misjudges the true nature of man. It involves a refusal to recognize what that nature really is.

"One cannot escape the impression that a good deal of modern philosophy, insofar as it excludes God, disallows a metaphysical interpretation and thus imposes a restriction on human experiences. In our view, not only the idea of God but belief in God too is present in the actions of men at their profoundest and most elementary level; for they evince precisely the qualities of trust and humility."[91] More even than certain forms of religiosity, atheism constitutes a dangerous alienation for man and creates a mental climate in which human endeavour, however worthy it may be in itself, is exposed to breakdown, enervation and total eclipse.

CONCLUSION

From all that has been said in the foregoing pages it has appeared in what directions Teilhard looked for a solution to the central problem that preoccupied him throughout his life: the problem of the relation between "love of God and love for the world". The data provided by the natural sciences, if properly interpreted, enabled us—he believed—to discover at a deeper level the principle governing cosmic evolution; and this made it possible to determine more closely the place and task of man within the greater whole. We live in an evolving world; and this process of evolution, in which everything is implicated, has a convergent character and is tending toward the realization of an ultimate unity. There is a fundamental harmony between a world so structured and a religion that not only offers the prospect of the world's eventual completion but sees that completion and unification as having a personal centre: the Omega point of history, the Christ who returns at the end of the Age. Such a religion, far from alienating us and seducing us from the business of living here on earth, can provide the supreme stimulus and consecration of our efforts to achieve progress in every sphere.

It cannot be the business of an "introduction" of this sort to offer a verdict on the work of Teilhard or on the various ideas and theories that he propounded in it. Our aim has been simply to give the reader opportunity to make some acquaintance with it, as well as to highlight its very considerable internal unity.

As we look back over the way we have come, it is clear that the work of this thinker is governed by two general presuppositions: first, that at the present stage of our knowledge of nature a synthetic interpretation—a phenomenology of the universe—is beginning to be possible and, secondly, that in the realm of action as well as of thought a synthesis is possible between religion and culture or—to state it more concretely—

between Christianity and the modern world view, with all that the latter involves.

Anyone who rejects those hypotheses will of course dismiss Teilhard's work as a whole—although such a person might well be able to concur with many of Teilhard's views and go along a good part of the way with him. But for anyone prepared to admit that the questions of a properly balanced world view and of a religious understanding of the world are undoubtedly legitimate questions—for such a person Teilhard's work can prove, as we think, to be valuable and helpful and indeed a worthy stimulus to further reflection on the subject. That is precisely how the author intended it, in the first instance, to be. As he saw it, we are not to regard his work as a *terminus ad quem* but rather as a point of departure. He knew very well that such a vast undertaking as the construction of a scientifically warrantable world view cannot be carried through by a single scientist, however comprehensive his knowledge might be—the more so because every way of representing reality can always be supplemented and improved on. Equally, he made allowance for the fact that a new theological synthesis which would take account not only of the new world view but also of new ideas in the fields of biblical criticism and philosophy is not going to appear suddenly from nowhere. St. Thomas Aquinas's *Summa* itself would not have been feasible apart from the work of his predecessors. But how could we ever hope to attain a new synthesis in all these areas, if we ruled out of court what was said and done by the forerunners and pioneers or rejected all their efforts as superfluous?

If it be asked, therefore, where the ultimate significance of his work is to be looked for, it could perhaps be replied that in the main—and leaving aside the undeniably brilliant insights which it contains—the real importance of his work lies in the tremendous power of inspiration which emanates from it. We are not far wide of the mark if we assert that Teilhard's primary intention was to show by what route it might be possible for us to arrive at a new unity in our thinking.

Professor Bernard Delfgaauw has justly observed in this connection: "A conception of this sort is open to attack on a
number of heads; but the crucial point is whether in its main
features it is acceptable and really does provide the lines on
which positive scientific, philosophical and theological enquiry can be co-ordinated. It is quite foolish to rush to the
support of Teilhard's theory with uncritical enthusiasm—and
just about as foolish to dismiss it out of hand. The only
sensible thing is to submit to searching examination the various
aspects and consequences of the theory in the fields of non-
speculative science, philosophy and theology".[1]

This work of submitting Teilhard's ideas to critical examination and argument is by now in full swing, and over a period
of several years has already given occasion for numerous
studies and fruitful confrontations; while on the other hand
the broad orientation of his thinking is having an effect on a
wide range of people and is forming a basis for discussion
among individuals representing the most disparate schools of
thought. The diffused influence of his ideas can hardly be
ignored or dismissed from the intellectual landscape of our
time; so that a historian of the modern outlook and cast of
mind can no more pass by him than by, say, Kierkegaard or
Nietzsche—and we all know how much their importance was
underestimated at first by the professional philosophers![2] To
what extent this influence of his will continue to spread and
his ideas remain an effective force is a question to which only
the future can supply the answer.

NOTES AND INDEX

INTRODUCTION

1 *Comment je crois*, 1934, pp. 1-2; (also in *Oeuvres* X).

2 " Heaven and World—these two, through complementary channels, have flowed together; and with the passing years I have been aware, with ever greater clarity and depth of feeling, of that confluence as the key to every advance—and, be it said, to every conflict too—in my inner life " (*Le Coeur de la Matière*, 1950, p. 24; also in *Oeuvres* X).

3 *Ce que le Monde attend en ce moment de l'Église de Dieu*, 1952, p.1.

4 *Le Coeur de la Matière*, p. 22; (also in *Oeuvres* X).

5 *L'Énergie Humaine* (*Oeuvres* VI), p. 101.

6 ". . . a struggle was joined within the very depths of my soul; for in my heart I knew that the cosmic sense and the Christic sense were present there together and that nothing could keep them apart " (*Le Coeur de la Matière*, p. 24).

7 ". . . 'cosmic sense' and 'Christic sense'—in me, two mutually quite independent axes, it would seem, in their birth and origin; and it was only at the cost of much time and effort that through and beyond the Human I was able eventually to grasp their connection, their convergence and, last of all, their fundamental identity " (*Ibid*, p.20).

8 ". . . a marvellous conjunction, no longer in a simple and confused way between Christ and Matter—but between a Christ perceived distinctly as *evolutive agent* and a positively recognized cosmic Centre of Evolution " (*Ibid.*, pp. 26-27).

9 Hermann Nohl, *Hegels theologische Jugendschriften*, Tübingen, 1907, p.28.

10 *Ibid.*, p.224.

11 *Le Milieu Divin* (English translation, London, Collins

and New York, Harper and Row, 1960, p.23; Fontana edition, 1964, p.53).

12   *La Vie Cosmique*, 1916, in *Écrits du Temps de la Guerre,* (Paris, Grasset, 1965, p.46); (English translation *Writings in Time of War,* London, Collins, and New York, Harper and Row, 1968).

13   *Ibid.*, p.46.

14   *Recherche, Travail et Adoration,* 1955, p. 4; (also in *Oeuvres* IX).

15   *Le Christique,* 1955, p. 8; (also in *Oeuvres* X).

16   *L'Activation de l'Énergie* (*Oeuvres* VII), p.404.

17   R. C. Kwant, *De Fenomenologie van Merleau-Ponty,* Utrecht-Antwerp, 1962, pp.15-16. An attempt to give more precise definition to Teilhard de Chardin's terminology has been made by Claude Cuénot (*Lexique Teilhard de Chardin,* Paris, Le Seuil, 1963).

18   *Informations Catholiques Internationales,* No. 111, 1 January, 1960, p.21.

19   *Ibid.*, p.15.

20   Jean Lacroix, *Le Sens de l'Athèisme Moderne* (Paris and Tournai, Casterman, 1959, p.28).

21   Gabriel Marcel, *Etre et Avoir,* Paris, 1935, pp.196-7. (English translation, *Being and Having,* London, Fontana edition, 1965, p.147.)

PART I

1 " Haec est ultima perfectio ad quam anima potest per-
venire, secundum philosophum, ut in ea describatur totus
ordo universi et causarum ejus." *De Veritate*, II.2.—
See Thomas Litt, *Les corps célestes dans l'Univers de
Saint Thomas d'Aquin*. Louvain-Paris 1963.

2 J. Huxley, *New Bottles for New Wine*, New York,
Harper and Row, 1957, p.41.

3 The bibliography of Teilhard. See further in this work.

4 In *Bulletin de la Société Géologique de France*, 6th
series, ¶ VII, 1957, p.798.

5 In *Encounter*, Vol. VI, April, 1956, pp.84-86.

6 *The Phenomenon of Man*, London, Collins, and New
York, Harper and Row, 1959, revised edition 1965,
p.29; Fontana edition, p.31.

7 On this see Claude Tresmontant, *Introduction à la Pensée
de Teilhard de Chardin*, Paris, Le Seuil, 1936, pp.19-24
(English translation *Pierre Teilhard de Chardin, His
Thought*, Baltimore, Helicon Press 1959) also P. Chauchard, *Man and Cosmos*, New York, Herder and Herder,
1965. " There is need of a synthesis of the sciences over
and above the individual branches of science, a synthesis
which will give us knowledge about ourselves and our
place in the universe . . . If it is true that synthesis is a
part of scientific work and comes within the reference
of science, it is no less true that the philosopher must
more than ever look to his role in the face of this synthesis, which, far from substituting for philosophy, necessitates, rather, a deepening of philosophical research "
(Chauchard, *op. cit.*, pp.35-36).

8 " However it may seem, the *Weltanschauung* that I am
proposing in no way represents a fixed and closed system.
There is no question here (such a thing would be ridicu-
lous) of a deductive world solution on the Hegelian
model, of a definitive plan of truth—but only of a
fascicle of *axes of progression* such as exist and are

gradually disclosed by every system in evolution. Not an exhaustive account of Truth, but lines of penetration by which there is opened up before our eyes an immeasurable field of as yet unexplored Reality " (*Comment je vois,* 1948, p.1; also in *Oeuvres* X).

9   C. d'Armagnac, " Philosophie de la nature et méthode chez le P. Teilhard de Chardin ", in *Archives de Philosophie,* Vol. XX, 1957, p.16.

10 A. Lalande, *Vocabulaire technique et critique de la Philosophie s.v. phénoménologie* : " Étude descriptive d'un ensemble de phénomènes ".

11 *The Phenomenon of Man,* pp.43-45.

12 A. de Waelhens, " Science, Phénoménologie, Ontologie ", in *Existence et Signification,* Louvain-Paris, Nauwelaerts, 1958, pp.105-121.

13 ". . . nothing is comprehensible except through its history." (*The Future of Man,* London, Collins, and New York, Harper and Row, 1964, p.12.)

14 " It is in the perception of this fundamental, dynamic unity that the modern advance in the idea of evolution essentially consists " (*l'Activation de l'Énergie,* Paris, Le Seuil, 1963, p.267; *Oeuvres* VII).

15 *The Vision of the Past,* London, Collins, and New York, Harper and Row, 1966, pp.245-247.

16 " *Die Evolution der Organismen* ", in : *Schöpfungsglaube und Evolutions-theorie: Eine Vortragsreihe,* Krönerverlag Stuttgart, 1955, p.53; see also G. Vandebroeck, *De oorsprong van de mens* (Logosreeks No. 7). Antwerp, 1955, p.9.

17 Pierre-P. Grassé, " Les mecanismes de l'Évolution " in : *Somme de médecine contemporaine,* Paris, La Diane Française, 1951, Vol. I, p.21.

18 L. Cuénot, *L'Évolution Biologique,* Paris, Masson, 1951. p.vi.

19 " Phenomenally speaking, the world presents itself to us not only as a system in simple motion, but as a system in a state of genesis—which is something quite different.

Through the metamorphoses of 'Matter', something comes into being (and simultaneously ceases to be) in accordance with a certain inclusive orientation, irrevocably and cumulatively. " *Le Christique*, p.3; (also in *Oeuvres* X).

20 "... there is a science of the universe without man. There is also a science of man as marginal to the universe; but there is not yet a science of the universe that embraces man as such." *The Vision of the Past*, London, Collins, and New York, Harper and Row, 1966, p.162.

21 See e.g., J. Piveteau, *Traité de Paléontologie*, Vol. VII, *Primates, Paléontologie humaine*, Paris, 1957. A summary yet very illuminating survey of the present position may be found in E. Boné, *Devenir de l'Homme*, Paris, Office Général du Livre, 1962.

22 "I am neither a philosopher nor a theologian, but a student of the ' phenomenon ', a physicist (natural philosopher) in the old Greek sense " (statement made during an interview; see *Nouvelles Littéraires*, 11 January 1951).

23 See e.g.: A. Dauvillier, *L'Origine photochimique de la vie* (Coll. Evolution des Sciences No. 11), Paris, Masson, 1958; H. Becher et al., *Vom Unbelebten zum Lebendigen* (Univ. Münster) Stuttgart, 1956; P. G. Fothergill, *Life and its Origin*, London, 1958; A. I. Oparin, *Die Entstehung des Lebens auf der Erde* (trans. from the Russian), Berlin, 1957.

24 *The Phenomenon of Man*, p.78.

25 *Ibid.*, p.102.

26 The problem of the source or origin of the human soul is not only one for natural science, but has philosophical and theological aspects too. To account for the origin of the soul, most Catholic theologians postulate a special intervention by God (see Encyclical *Humani Generis*, Acta Apostolicae Sedis, Rome, 1950, p.575); their primary purpose in so doing is to emphasize that the origin of man cannot be attributed to accident and that each man has a unique status as an individual person. Here we are

concerned only with the phenomenological aspect of the problem.

27 *The Phenomenon of Man*, pp.165-6.

28 *Ibid.*, p.167.

29 *Ibid.*, p.167.

30 *Ibid.*, p.174.

31 *Ibid.*, p.165.

32 *Ibid.*, p.177.

33 *Ibid.*, p.49.

34 F. M. Bergounioux, *La Préhistoire et Ses Problèmes*, Paris, Fayard, 1958, p.367.

35 This view is propounded at some length by Professor P. Chauchard (himself a neurophysiologist), who concludes as follows : " The idea of a scientific aspect of consciousness, while rejected alike by most scientists and philosophers in their refusal to recognize the connection between the materially objective and the spiritually subjective in the organic unit, is inevitable and inescapably posited by the discoveries of the psychobiological sciences." (*Man and Cosmos*, p.84).

36 " In his law of complexity-consciousness, Teilhard describes reality as it appears in terms of a scientific explanation. There is no denying it, and it is very important to understand it and then see what there is of it that philosophy must retain." (*Man and Cosmos*, p.85).

37 *The Phenomenon of Man*, p.57, footnote 1.

38 *Ibid.*, p.60.

39 *Ibid.*, p.60.

40 *Ibid.*, p.60-61.

41 *Ibid.*, p.55.

42 *Ibid.*, *loc. cit.*

43 Cf. Julian Huxley, *The Uniqueness of Man*, London, 1941, ch. 1.

44 *Le Christ Évoluteur*, p.2 (*Cahiers Pierre Teilhard de Chardin*, No. 5).

45 *Ibid.*, p.2.

46 *Letters from a Traveller,* London, Collins, and New York, Harper and Row, 1962, p.207.

47 *The Future of Man,* p.227.

48 *The Appearance of Man,* p.244.

49 *La Vie Cosmique,* p.131 (*Écrits du Temps de la Guerre,* p.23).

50 "Evolution, by the very mechanism of its syntheses, charges itself with an ever-growing measure of freedom" (*The Future of Man,* p.72).

51 "Zoologically speaking, mankind offers us the unique spectacle of a 'species' capable of achieving something in which all previous species had failed. It has succeeded, not only in becoming cosmopolitan, but in stretching a single organised membrane over the earth without breaking it" (*The Phenomenon of Man,* pp.241-242).

52 "It is not merely a matter of the machine which liberates, relieving both individual and collective thought of the trammels which hinder its progress, but also of the machine which creates, helping to assemble, and to concentrate in the form of an ever more deeply penetrating organism, all the reflective elements upon earth" (*The Future of Man,* p.167).—"In its progress through a million centuries, mounting from the depths of the unconscious to consciousness, when has Life proceeded otherwise than by releasing psychic forces through the medium of the mechanisms it has devised?" (*Ibid.,* p.171).—See also *L'Activation de l'Énergie* (*Oeuvres* VII), pp. 159-169.

53 "The processes of chemistry and biology are continued without a break in the social sphere" (*The Future of Man,* p.131).

54 "What is really going on, under cover and in the form of human collectivization, is the super-organisation of Matter upon itself, which as it continues to advance produces its habitual, specific effect, the further liberation of consciousness" (*Ibid.,* p.132).

55 "However personal and incommunicable it may be at its

root and origin, Reflection can only be developed in communion with others. It is essentially a social phenomenon " (*Ibid.*, p.133).

56 " We can progress only by uniting: this . . . is the law of
Life" (*Ibid.*, p.74); " True union, the union of heart
and spirit, does not enslave, nor does it neutralise the
individuals which it brings together. It *super-personalises*
them" (*Ibid.*, p.119); " Love has always been carefully
eliminated from realist and positivist concepts of the
world; but sooner or later we shall have to acknowledge
that it is the fundamental impulse of Life, or, if you
prefer, the one natural medium in which the rising course
of evolution can proceed. With love omitted there is
truly nothing ahead of us except the forbidding prospect
of standardisation and enslavement—the doom of ants
and termites. It is through love and within love that we
must look for the deepening of our deepest self, in the
life-giving coming together of human kind. Love is the
free and imaginative outpouring of the spirit over all
unexplored paths. It links those who love in bonds that
unite but do not confound, causing them to discover in
their mutual contact an exaltation capable, incomparably
more than any arrogance of solitude, of arousing in the
heart of their being all that they possess of uniqueness
and creative power" (*Ibid.*, pp.54-55).

57 " Thus socialisation, whose hour seems to have sounded
for Mankind, does not by any means signify the ending
of the Era of the Individual upon earth, but far more its
beginning" (*Ibid.*, p.54); " Where Man is concerned,
therefore, collectivisation, super-socialisation, can signify
nothing other than super-personalisation " (*Super-humanité, Super-Christ, Super-charité*, 1934, p.6; in *Science et
Christ, Oeuvres* IX, 1965).

58 " The forms of the future are *ipso facto* not foreseeable.
. . . The problem we set ourselves is merely that of
knowing in which direction, along what lines, the meta-

morphosis of man is taking effect" (*Réflexions sur la Crise Présente*, 1937, p.11).

59 See *The Future of Man*, pp.120-123.

60 ". . . looking far ahead we may descry an ultimate state in which, organically associated with one another (*more closely* than the cells of a single brain) we shall form in our entirety a single system, ultra-complex and, in consequence, ultra-centrated" (*Ibid.*, p.89).

61 Teilhard does not think that the future course of evolution is likely to bring with it any further appreciable change of a morphological character in the human species : " To all appearance the ultimate perfection of the human *element* was achieved many thousands of years ago, which is to say that the individual instrument of thought and action may be considered to have been finalised " (*Ibid.*, p.16); " It is not to the idea of anatomically super-cerebralised individuals but to that of super-socialised groupings that we must look, if we want to make a scientific prediction as to what Super-Humanity will be like" (*Super-humanité, Super-Christ, Super-charité*, p.6; also in *Oeuvres* IX).

62 See *The Future of Man*, pp.286-287.

63 *L'Esprit de la Terre*, 1931, p.7; (also in *L'Énergie Humaine, Oeuvres* VI, 1962).

64 ". . . the movement of the cosmos towards the highest degree of consciousness . . . represents the essence of biological evolution " (*The Future of Man*, p.67).

65 *The Phenomenon of Man*, p.168; ". . . the genesis of spirit is a cosmic phenomenon; and the cosmos consists in this very genesis " (*L'Esprit de la Terre*, p.8; also in *Oeuvres* VI); " Cosmogenesis is essentially a ' noo-genesis ' " (Letter of 26th January, 1954, cited by C. Cuénot, *Pierre Teilhard de Chardin: Les Grandes Étapes de son Évolution*, Paris, Plon, 1958, p.449; English translation *Teilhard de Chardin: A Biographical Study*, London, Burns & Oates, Baltimore, Helicon Press, 1965, p.369).

66   *The Phenomenon of Man*, p.246.

67   "... the vast and extreme organicity of the universe as a whole, considered in terms of its internal forces of development" (*The Future of Man*, p.285).

68   On this see: Georges Morel, "Karl Marx et le P. Teilhard de Chardin", in *Études*, Vol. 304 (January 1960), pp.80-87.

69   "Within the Spirit of man, as within some unique and irreplaceable fruit, is gathered up the whole sublimated Life—in short, the whole cosmic import—of the Earth" (*L'Esprit de la Terre*, p.15; also in *Oeuvres* VI).

70   *The Observer*, 22 November 1959.

71   R.-M. Albérès, *Jean-Paul Sartre*, pp.13-14 (Paris, Éditions Universitaires, 1958).—Simone de Beauvoir wrote of Sartre: "He was allergic to leaf-green, could not abide the sheer greenness of the open fields, could only put up with it so long as he could forget all about it" (*La Force de l'Age*, Paris, 1960, p.17).

72   "... those who are faithful to Earth ..." (*The Future of Man*, p.44); "... remain faithful to the call of the cosmos ..." (*La Vie Cosmique*, 1916, p.15; also in *Écrits du Temps de la Guerre*).

PART II

1 *Recherche, Travail et Adoration,* 1955, p.1; (also in *Oeuvres* IX).

2 Letter of 1 January, 1954; see C. Cuénot *op. cit.* p.482; English translation, p.400.

3 *Christianisme et Évolution,* 1945, p.1; (also in *Oeuvres* XI).

4 *Quelques réflexions sur la Conversion du Monde,* 1936, pp.2-3; (also in *Oeuvres* IX).

5 F. Gonseth in his preface to G. Lemaître, *L'Hypothèse de l'Atome Primitif,* Neuchâtel-Brussels, 1946, p.17.

6 *L'Incroyance Moderne,* 1933. pp.1-2; (also in *Oeuvres* IX).

7 *Christianisme et Évolution,* p.2; (also in *Oeuvres* XI).

8 Letter of 10 December, 1952. See *Cuénot, op. cit.,* p.448; English translation, p.368.

9 *L'Activation de l'Énergie (Oeuvres* VII), p.406.

10 Jean Lacroix, *Le Sens de l'Athéisme Moderne,* Paris and Tournai, Casterman, 1959, pp.24-25.

11 Francis Jeanson, *Lignes de Départ,* Paris Éditions du Seuil, 1963, p.185.—" To the eyes of anyone who has ever had brought home to him the sheer fact of human misery, Christianity can only appear, from a *sociological* standpoint, in the guise of a pretty shocking mystification " *(Ibid.,* p.93).

12 A. Dondeyne, *Foi Chrétienne et Pensée Contemporaine,* Louvain-Paris, 1952, p.11.

13 *Quelques Réflexions sur la Conversion du Monde,* p.3; (also in *Oeuvres* IX).

14 *Ibid.,* pp.3-4.

15 *L'Incroyance Moderne,* p.2 (also in *Oeuvres* IX).

16 Letter of 10 January, 1953. See *Cuénot, op. cit.,* p.442; English translation, p.363.

17 *Note pour servir à l'Évangélisation des Temps Nouveaux,*

1920, p.2; (*Écrits du Temps de la Guerre*, p.363).

18 *L'Incroyance Moderne.* p.2.—See also: *Le Sens Humain*, 1929, p.9: "The truth is that if Christianity to-day no longer appeals, that is not at all because it is too hard and too high (as its champions claim to believe), but on the contrary because its ideal seems neither pure enough nor lofty enough. As it is currently presented, the Christian religion would appear to constrict the mind and stifle the heart."

19 *Ce que le Monde attend en ce moment de l'Église de Dieu*, 1952, p.1.

20 *Ibid.*, p.3.

21 See in this connection the testimony of Pierre Leroy in *Teilhard de Chardin tel que je l'ai connu*, Paris, Plon, 1958—and especially the letter of 12 October, 1951, quoted on pp.55-60; (English translation in *Letters from a Traveller*, pp.41-44 and *Le Milieu Divin*, Fontana, pp.37-40).

22 *Informations Catholiques Internationales*, No. 132, 15 November, 1960, p.14.

23 It is clear from various letters and notes just how greatly Newman was interested in Darwin's theory—and particularly in connection with the theological issues which it raised. "I cannot imagine," he wrote, ". . . why Darwinism should be considered inconsistent with Catholic doctrine" (document A.18.21 at the Birmingham Oratory). Nor did he fail to notice the implications of the idea of evolution for philosophy: ". . . I saw that the principle of development not only accounted for certain facts, but was in itself a remarkable philosophical phenomenon" (*Apologia pro Vita Sua*, standard ed., Longman, p.198). He further observed: "There is as much want of simplicity in the idea of distinct species as in that of the creation of trees in full growth, or of rocks with fossils in them. I mean that it is as strange that monkeys should be so like men, with no *historical* connection between them, as that there should be no course of facts by which

fossil bones got into rocks. The one idea stands to the
other as fluxions to differentials . . . I will either go
the whole hog with Darwin, or, dispensing with time and
history altogether, hold, not only the theory of distinct
species but that also of the creation of fossil-bearing
rocks " (*Sundries,* p.83—See also Culler, *The Imperial
Intellect,* p.267).—On 5 April 1878 Mark Pattison
wrote to Newman : " Is it not a remarkable thing that you
should have first started the idea—and the word—
Development, as the key to the history of Church doctrine : and since then it has gradually become the domin-
ant idea of all history, biology, physics, and in short has
metamorphosed our view of every science, and of all
knowledge. . . ." (Birmingham Oratory. Letters from
and to Pattison) (from notes and memoranda supplied by
Dr. Zeno). It may be recalled that Newman's *Essay on
the Development of Christian Doctrine* appeared in 1845.
Darwin's *The Origin of Species* came out in 1859.

24 Jean Guitton, *Journal, Études et Rencontres,* Paris, Plon,
    1959, p.231 (English translation *The Guitton Journals,*
    London, Harvill, 1963, p.246).

25 A. Hulsbosch, *De Schepping Gods: Schepping, zonde en
    verlossing in het evolutionistische wereldbeeld,* Roer-
    mond-Maaseik, 1963, p.9.

26 Letter of 1 January, 1951. See C. Cuénot, *op. cit.,* p.330,
    note 3; English translation, p.273.

27 *Le Milieu Divin,* Fontana edition, p.43.

28 *Note pour servir à l'Évangélisation des Temps Nouveaux,*
    p.8.

29 *Ibid.,* p.6.—See also : *Note sur le Christ Universel,* 1920,
    p.3; (also in *Oeuvres* IX).

30 Ephes. 3.8.

31 See C. Cuénot, *op. cit.,* p.330.

32 *Comment je vois,* 1948, p.25; (also in *Oeuvres* X).

33 *Comment je crois,* 1934, p.31; (also in *Oeuvres* X).

34 *Summa theologica,* III, 9.1., art. 3 : *Utrum, si homo non*

peccasset, Deus incarnatus fuisset (Whether, if man had not sinned, God would have become incarnate).

35 Col. 1.18.

36 E. Schillebeeckx, "*De zin van het mens-zijn van Jezus, de Christus*", in *Tijdschrift voor Theologie*, 2nd Vol., 1962, p.168.

37 *Christianisme et Évolution*, 1945, p.3; (also in *Oeuvres* XI).

38 *Note sur le Christ Universel*, p.1; (also in *Oeuvres* IX).

39 *Christianisme et Évolution*, p.3; (also in *Oeuvres* XI).

40 Teilhard sometimes made explicit reference to the Scotist view of the matter; see: *Esquisse d'une dialectique de l'Esprit* in *L'Activation de l'Énergie*, p.158. (*Oeuvres* VII); not to mention any specific further instances.

41 *Le Christ Évoluteur*, 1942, p.4 (*Cahiers Pierre Teilhard de Chardin*, 5, Ed. du Seuil, Paris).

42 *Super-humanité, Super-Christ, Super-charité*, 1943, p.9.

43 See Mgr. L. Cerfaux, *Le Christ dans la Théologie de Saint-Paul*, Paris, Ed. du Cerf, 1951: "Thus we notice in the Epistles of the captivity a tendency . . . to extend Christ's pleroma, that is to say the sphere within which the writ of his authority runs, to the cosmos" (p.322). —"All things have been created by him; and they are created for him, they tend toward him, in order through him to realize their end, which is to make God manifest" (p.323).—"Although the primary intention has been frustrated, the Christ is still he in whom all things cohere, and on whom they depend (to whom they are subject), with an intrinsic dependence; no creature can escape from his domain" (*ibid.*). (English translation, *The Church in the Theology of St. Paul*, New York, Herder and Herder, 1959).

44 *L'Énergie Humaine*, p.113 (*Oeuvres* VI).

45 *Super-humanité, Super-Christ, Super-charité*, p.9.

46 *Christianisme et Évolution*, p.6; (also in *Oeuvres* XI).

47 C. Cuénot, *op. cit.*, p.450; English translation, p.370.

48 Col. 1.16.

49 Col. 1.17.
50 I Cor. 3.23.
51 *Christologie et Évolution,* 1933, p.9; (also in *Oeuvres XI).*
52 *Ibid.*
53 *Trois Choses que je vois,* 1948, p.7.
54 *Ibid.,* pp.8-9.
55 I Cor. 15.28.—See : *Introduction à la Vie Chrétienne,* 1944, p.1; (also in *Oeuvres* XI).
56 *Le Coeur de la Matière,* 1950, p.29; (also in *Oeuvres* X).
57 *Le Christique,* 1955, p.9; (also in *Oeuvres* X).
58 For a full treatment of this see M. Barthélemy-Madaule, *Bergson et Teilhard de Chardin,* Paris, Le Seuil, 1963, pp.411-421; 431-440. H. de Lubac, *The Religion of Teilhard de Chardin,* London, Collins, New York, Desclée, 1967; 1962, pp.36-55 et passim; P. Smulders, *Het visioen van Teilhard de Chardin,* Bruges, Desclée de Brouwer, 1962, pp.202-271; (English translation *The Design of Teilhard de Chardin,* Westminster, Newman, 1967).
59 *Comment je vois,* p.33; (also in *Oeuvres* X).
60 *Christologie et Évolution,* p.7; (also in *Oeuvres* XI).
61 Olivier Rabut, O.P., *Dialogue with Teilhard de Chardin,* London, Sheed and Ward, 1961, pp.186-7.
62 *Ce que le Monde attend en ce moment de l'Église de Dieu,* p.5.
63 *L'Activation de l'Énergie,* p.404 *(Oeuvres* VII).
64 *Comment je crois,* pp.40-41; (also in *Oeuvres* X).
65 *Trois Choses que je vois,* p.7.
66 Rabut, *op. cit.,* p.172.
67 *The Phenomenon of Man,* p.298.
68 *Comment je vois,* p.28; (also in *Oeuvres* X).
69 *Ibid.,* p.39.
70 *Le Milieu Divin,* p.23, Fontana edition, p.53.
71 Gen. 1.28.
72 *Le Milieu Divin,* p.35, Fontana edition, p.63.
73 *Comment je crois,* p.40; (also in *Oeuvres* X).

74   Letter to Père A. Valensin, cited in *Le Milieu Divin*, p.74, Fontana edition, p.93.
75   *Comment je crois*, p.49; (also in *Oeuvres* X).
76   *Chistologie et Évolution*, p.12; (also in *Oeuvres* XI).
77   *Note sur la notion de perfection chrétienne*, 1942, p.4.
78   *La Parole Attendue*, 1940, pp.4-5.
79   *L'Énergie Humaine* (*Oeuvres* VI), pp.221-2.
80   *Le Sens Humain*, 1929, p.6.
81   *Ibid.*, p.11.
82   *The Future of Man*, p.154.
83   *L'Énergie Humaine* (*Oeuvres* VI), p.134.
84   *La Parole Attendue*, p.3.
85   *Christologie et Évolution*, pp.11-12; (also in *Oeuvres* XI).
86   *L'Énergie Humaine* (*Oeuvres* VI), p.136.
87   C. Cuénot, *op. cit.*, p.457; English translation, p.377.
88   *Ce que le Monde attend en ce moment de l'Église de Dieu*, p.3.
89   P. Chauchard, "Teilhard de Chardin, l'humanisme socialiste et la réconciliation des Humanismes", in *Synthèses*, No. 169-170, 1960, p.331.
90   Lacroix, *Le Sens de l'Athéisme Moderne*, p.65.
91   *Ibid.*, p.61.

CONCLUSION

1 Bernard Delfgaauw, *Teilhard de Chardin*, Baarn, Het Wereldvenster, 1961, p.35. (London, Collins, and New York, Harper and Row, 1968).

2 " Could one conceive of a history of modern philosophy that made no reference to Nietzsche? But then it would be difficult to claim that Teilhard is an event of less importance for our time that Nietzsche was for his " (André George, in *Nouvelles Littéraires,* 29 August 1963).

INDEX

activity, human; divinization 150-4; value 125
Albérès, R. M. 107
anthropogenesis 135 149 160 163
Aristotle 37
Armagnac, Christian d' 51
astronomy 58 88 90
atheism 23 114-5 163
atoms 67 68 74 97 98
Augustine, St. 21 122

Bergounioux, F. M. 75-6
Bergson, Henri 103 139
Bertalanffy, L. 60
biogenesis 139 142
biology 58 77 90
biosphere 65-6 91 92
birds 65
Black, Davidson 43
boredom of living 153 163
Buddhism 24 102

Calvo-Serer 85
Cambrian age 65
cells 74 98
cerebralization 74
Chauchard, Paul 159 171 174
chemistry 88
Chenu, M. D. 31
Christ 117 128 131 140; Alpha and Omega 132 133; the Christic 140; cosmic function 23 129-30 131-2 133-4 136-9 145 182; the evolver 140; function identical with Omega 134-5 137-9 142 151; historic 135-7; kingship 131 134; meaning of history 148; place in evolving creation 134 169; return 128 135 138 140-1; Super- 140; total 147-8; universal 137 140 153; and world 124 131. *See* Christogenesis, Incarnation, Omega.
Christianity: eschatological character 135-6; ethics 128; and modern man 116-9 179-80; and modern world 30; phenomenological analysis 127-9; and science 123; synthesis with Teilhard's world view 146 164-5; vitality 127
Christians: and new religion 118-9; and new scientific perspectives 117-8
Christic consciousness 23 169
Christification 142
Christique, Le 26
Christogenesis 137 139 142 146 149 163
Christology 124 135
Church: and modern thought 155-6; place of 148-9; resistance to expansion of 118; ultra-socialization 149
Coeur de la Matière, Le 26-7
complexity, increasing 73-7 81 100
complexity-consciousness, law of 74-9 93 100 174
consciousness 77; communal 96 100-1; degrees of 78-9; reflective 70-1 80 81; scientific aspect 174; self- 74; and super-organization of matter 97 175
continuity, discontinuity in 71
Copernicus 38
cosmic consciousness 23 169